Raising NLD Superstars

Raising NLD Superstars

What Families with Nonverbal Learning Disabilities Need to Know About Nurturing Confident, Competent Kids

Marcia Brown Rubinstien

Foreword by Pamela B. Tanguay

Jessica Kingsley Publishers
London and Philadelphia

Cover artwork by Jane W. Maciel

First published in 2005
by Jessica Kingsley Publishers
116 Pentonville Road
London N1 9JB, UK
and
400 Market Street, Suite 400
Philadelphia, PA 19106, USA

www.jkp.com

Copyright © Marcia Brown Rubinstien 2005
Foreword copyright © Pamela B. Tanguay 2005
Illustrations copyright © Jane W. Maciel 2005

Library of Congress Cataloging in Publication Data
Rubinstien, Marcia Brown, 1947-
Raising NLD superstars : what families with nonverbal learning disorders need to know about nurturing confident, competent kids / Marcia Brown Rubinstien ; foreword by Pamela Tanguay.— 1st American pbk.
    p. cm.
Includes bibliographical references and index.
ISBN 1-84310-770-8 (pbk.)
    1. Nonverbal learning disabilities. 2. Learning disabled children. 3. Parents of children with disabilities. 4. Child rearing. I. Title.
    RJ506.L4R82 2004
    618.92'85889—dc22
                                                    2004010971

British Library Cataloguing in Publication Data
A CIP catalogue record for this book is available from the British Library

ISBN-13: 978 1 84310 770 5
ISBN-10: 1 84310 770 8

Printed and Bound in Great Britain by
Athenaeum Press, Gateshead, Tyne and Wear

Contents

Acknowledgments

Without the support and encouragement of my dear friends and the long-suffering members of my family, this book would still be drifting aimlessly among my dendrites. Endless doses of love and support helped me transform the amorphous mass of what experience has taught me into an orderly account of what I hope can enlighten others. Tangible, visible thanks to Jane Maciel, whose illustrations enliven my words with images of graphic delight.

Special thanks to my husband who probably hopes that I'll be more subdued and better organized in the next thirty years of our life together. I can only ask that he wait around to see.

Despite the devotion of many, my true inspiration throughout this process has been my youngest son, Amiel, who was diagnosed at the age of seven as a gifted child with a nonverbal learning disorder. Very little was known about NLD when he was first diagnosed in 1992, though our entire family was affected by the pain and frustration he encountered at the hands of ignorant and inflexible educators.

Over the years, he suffered stoically through epithets of "lazy" and "oppositional." Just a year before graduating from high school, his neuro-psychologist advised us that he would probably never have the organizational skills to live an independent life at college. First we cried. Then we did what all parents should do when they receive a report with which they don't agree. We got a second opinion – our own.

The completion of these pages coincides with the triumphant completion of our son's first semester in college. It is my hope that the anecdotes, guidelines, and suggestions in this book can bring others with NLD in the family to the celebration of similar success. As I write of the possibility, he exemplifies the actuality.

By learning more about successful interventions for the complex syndrome of NLD, I hope that each parent, friend, family member, or caregiver who reads this book can experience the joy of seeing another NLDer approach adulthood with the skills for independence and productivity.

This book is for you, Ami, with love.

Foreword

Ten years ago, information on nonverbal learning disorder (NLD), also referred to as nonverbal learning disabilities, was almost nonexistent. The only meaningful publication on the disorder was written by Dr. Byron Rourke in 1989, and focused primarily on the definition and implications of NLD. Although very comprehensive, his book was targeted to professionals, and was therefore difficult for the lay person to read and comprehend.

Parents of children with NLD have been frustrated by the fact that, once a diagnosis was made, there was precious little written on how to help the child. Over the past decade, information has begun to trickle into the hands of professionals and, more recently, parents. Parents in particular have gobbled up these books hoping to find intervention strategies which might lead to a path of more neurologically typical development for their NLD child. With the exception of a few, most have failed to deliver what parents so desperately need – specific "hands on" guidance on how to help their child.

In this refreshing new book, it is clear from page one that the author has an intimate understanding of NLD, as well as how it affects not only the child, but the entire family. The first two chapters present a very "user friendly" explanation of the disorder, and how to secure a diagnosis. The author's explanation of the diagnostic process, the tests which may be administered and what they measure, all help to demystify the evaluation process, as well as help the reader to grasp the implications of this low incidence disability. While reading these first chapters, you may be thinking "…okay, okay, I know all that, but where's the beef?" The "beef" begins in Chapter 3, and from that point on, you will find it difficult to put this book down.

The author brings a unique perspective to the NLD table. She is both an educator and a parent of an NLD child. Her experience and good sense is evident on each and every page. Drawing from her work with not only her own NLD son but her numerous clients who share this disorder, the author provides a wealth of knowledge with both wit and compassion, addressing even the most awkward topics, as in the following excerpt:

> Occupational therapists can explain that there are two areas on our bodies which contain the most sensory endings. One is the scalp, which usually don't present much of a problem in public, unless it is hosting colonies of creatures not normally expected to reside in that habitat. A boy who scratches his head in public, unless the scratching is related to the aforementioned visitors, is not likely to be considered socially inappropriate. The other repository of multiple endings is the genital area. Most children find out about this sensory subsidy while still in diapers, if not before.

> Boys, perhaps because their apparatus is so accessible, often develop the habit of making sure that everything is in the right place and of giving a few manly scratches for a positive sensory experience. As they mature, however, there are complications attached to genital sensory pleasure, and some adolescents find it rather important to check on the equipment with little regard for appropriateness of time or place. If your son has been wearing boxer shorts because they offer minimal contact with his body and minimal possibility of sensory discomfort, you might want to suggest that he is no longer anatomically suited for free-form and accessible underwear.

The author does a remarkable job of providing incredible substance, while not overwhelming or depressing the reader. No fluff here – just page after page of useful information, presented by a very talented writer whose passion for our unique children comes through loud and clear.

Do not walk, but run to your local book store to get a copy of this marvelous new resource.

Pamela B. Tanguay, author of Nonverbal Learning Disabilities at Home: A Parent's Guide *and* Nonverbal Learning Disabilities at School: Educating Students with NLD, Asperger Syndrome, and Related Conditions, *and owner of NLD on the Web! (http://www.nldontheweb.org)*

Introduction

Our oldest son was born with astonishing beauty, charm, and passion. However, he has never been able to connect an action with its logical outcome. When he was two years old, he dove into the deep end of a pool before having enjoyed the benefit of swimming lessons. Twenty-eight years later, his journey to manhood has been marked with similar grandiose gestures and some equally frightening rescues. The sudden onset of epilepsy at age twelve merely fortified his bravado and reinforced his determination to take the risk first and consider the consequence later.

When our second son was born two years later, we were somewhat startled by the alertness of his large brown eyes as they scanned and analyzed the neonatal unit and all visitors with an almost preternatural intelligence. Nevertheless, having lived through trial by fire with our first-born, my husband and I thought we were somewhat prepared for all the possibilities of parenthood. It is hard to surmise, however, what a child with an astronomic IQ and boundless physical energy can imagine. At the age of three, this child decided to ride his bicycle down four flights of stairs. Unable to stop his trajectory, we breathed a sigh of relief as the two flying objects disconnected and he arrived safely on the first-floor landing. Moments later, however, the bicycle crashed into him, breaking his arm. Now an adult, he has

continued to live life in a similar manner, including the choice to treat his severe asthma by living in the cleanest air in the United States, fourteen thousand feet straight up.

When our daughter was born, I must admit that some foolish, sexist images of a sweet and gentle being in pigtails still persisted in the cobwebs of my mind. Well, the pigtails did materialize – at least for the short time that I was in control of her shiny dark hair. But she walked at eight months and has been fiercely independent ever since. In a world filled with music, dance, and poetry, she excels as a scholar and friend. And, not surprisingly, her approach to the world is no different from the one she has used at our dinner table since the moment she learned to hold a spoon. "No thanks, Mom, I'll serve myself."

Into this complicated but committed clan, our fourth child was born. His siblings had mixed reactions to the addition. Both brothers were delighted with the additional dose of testosterone into the family, but our daughter was horrified that we would even go to the trouble of bringing home another boy from the hospital. Even the Cabbage Patch Kid we gave her to mother was little compensation. She was soon making helpful suggestions such as "When we're finished with him, we could put him in the garbage." At five, our daughter was immune to the velvety allure of baby cheeks. She was acutely aware, however, that people were not stopping by the house simply to see how adorable she looked in her tutu.

At 38, I assumed I had mastered the skills of mothering and had been rewarded with the perfect child. Gentle and quiet, the fourth child nursed without distraction, never practiced for the Olympic Gymnastics team while I changed his diaper, and seemed to enjoy all the ministrations of bubble bath, lotion, massage, and Mommy that I could invent. He sat contently as I shuffled the others along to their myriad activities. All of the carpool kids enjoyed his demeanor and his presence in the omnipresent carseat. Before he was a year old, he was speaking in full sentences. Since we had already assumed he was a genius, this merely confirmed our suspicion.

One day a friend sent her husband over with a load of sopping wet laundry after a domestic dryer disaster. Confronting a model quite different from his own in the laundry room next to our kitchen, our bewildered neighbor asked, "How does this work?" Number Four was busily eating

Cheerios from the tray of his high chair. Suddenly a diminutive voice piped up. "Just pick up the lid and read the 'constructions'," he advised, with more than a little disdain. Both of us stared at him in disbelief. He was eleven months old. He didn't walk until much later than his siblings, but I never worried. I just assumed he was conserving all of his energy for his mouth!

When our youngest was two, we traveled to Israel and Europe to celebrate his oldest brother's Bar Mitzvah. Traveling abroad with four children is not a vacation. It is work. The older three presented challenges we had never anticipated. But unexpectedly, the baby was a total delight. He sat quietly in his stroller and took in the sights like a senior citizen on a tour bus. In the hotel, he played quietly in his portable playpen and never seemed interested in escaping or exploring. At family gatherings, he allowed himself to be passed around like a ripe juicy melon in an open air market. All of the relatives remarked on his exceptional nature. Eleven years later, when we returned for his own Bar Mitzvah, their remarks would be devastatingly different.

We know today that these infant and toddler behaviors showed evidence of the neurophysiological syndrome called nonverbal learning disorder or NLD. His precocious vocabulary development, lack of exploratory behavior in infancy, and relatively delayed psychomotor skills are part of a configuration of symptoms that should have alerted his pediatrician to the possibility of a right hemisphere disorder. But little was known about NLD in 1985, when he was born, and until his differences became too obvious to overlook, we simply assumed that he was a quirky little genius who would probably never be picked for the NBA. With early diagnosis and intervention, he might have been spared not only a difficult passage into adolescence, but also the burdens of clinical depression, low self-esteem, sensory defensiveness, and severe anxiety.

The formal diagnosis of NLD is generally made according to categories defined by Dr. Byron Rourke, but there is enormous variation even among those who match the diagnostic classifications to a tee. Specialists ruefully agree, "When you've seen one individual with NLD, you've seen *one* individual with NLD!"

An ingrown toenail or a ruptured eardrum is symptomatically characteristic to the professional trained to diagnose and treat it. Though the individual suffering may experience various levels of discomfort, the boundaries and symptoms are clear. In all but the most unusual cases, these characteristic ailments respond to predetermined treatment or medication.

NLD, however, is a disorder which extends far beyond the right hemisphere of the brain, where it is thought to originate. The syndrome is directly affected by interaction with environment and experience. Although this susceptibility to external factors can complicate both the diagnosis and the presentation, it can also offer the hope of positive change through appropriate intervention. Moreover, NLD is a syndrome of assets and deficits. If we can encourage those who carry the diagnosis to maximize their assets and downplay the deficits, perhaps clinicians and psychologists can predict a brighter future for people diagnosed with NLD.

This book is intended as a guide for families living with NLD. It should be read by parents, siblings, and friends who have trouble understanding why Danny won't wear scratchy denim jeans or why Dana isn't really interested in jumping Double Dutch. It can help you understand what issues are important to your child and where you should take a stand against manipulation or despair. It is intended to acknowledge the needs of people with NLD while at the same time validating the feelings of those who live with them and care for them. Like any type of learning disability, NLD is a family affair. Even when only one member has the diagnosis, everyone must adjust to the demands it makes on the entire family.

Finally, kids with NLD are, first and foremost, kids. They can be sweet or sassy, exemplary or evil, kind or cantankerous. Sometimes, it's not the NLD; it's just plain kid! But before you turn the page to learn about understanding kids with NLD, you have a far more important task to accomplish. You must learn to love them.

Chapter One

Getting the Diagnosis

A ren't family reunions wonderful? Teenagers check out which cousins are hot and which are not, while relations of all degrees marvel at how they could have produced such intelligent, good-looking progeny despite the evident gene pool contributed by the other side. Middleaged matrons surreptitiously measure whose waist has gone to waste, while males of all generations anxiously approximate hairlines, hoping to find genetic proof that male pattern baldness is only an occasional aberration.

Feeling somewhat relieved that you are related to this eclectic assortment by marriage only, you gather information for the next time your spouse huffs and puffs at a child's behavior. One day, when asked "Honestly, dear, can't you manage to control what your son does?" you will now be able to reply archly, "But, darling, he reminds me almost exactly of your favorite great-uncle Randy! Surely you remember how he stowed away on a tramp steamer at 14 until he found out that wasn't why they called it a tramp steamer?"

Casting future problems aside, you amble over to the sandbox to watch a coterie of cousins garnish themselves with grime. Some are building castles. Some are dumping pails. Others have developed elaborate waterways and cloverleafs. But your pride and joy, who has just turned six, is discoursing to a group of toddlers whose diapers are so filled with sand that they are rooted to the spot. With great attention to detail and little to the fact that he has lost the interest of even this captive audience, Chester is lecturing on the larval stages of the banded hairstreak caterpillar. For a moment, you don't know whether to experience pride or panic. This is definitely not typical behavior, even for cousins his age on the "other" side. Could he be an incipient genius, or could something truly bizarre be going on in his brain?

Meanwhile, miles away, the issue of another illustrious family (is it possible that some of those genes could be yours?), is also puzzling her parents. Cadence had done nicely in a small elementary school where no one minded her arcane interests, her eccentric style of dress, or her idiosyncratic manner of processing information. But in the larger public middle school, Cadence is out of step with the beat. Completing her homework is not a problem, because she can't even begin! Before long, Cadence begins to suffer from excruciating stomach aches, coughs, and exotic maladies that afflict her virulently every weekday morning and vanish almost as quickly as the exhaust fumes of the departing school bus.

Carson, on the other hand, has school down to a science. And for that matter, a math, social studies, and language arts, too. He has notebooks, file systems, and buddy-net homework lines set up for each class. He checks his backpack at night before going to bed and several times before leaving for school. In fact, he found himself worrying so much about these things that he really couldn't go on to other things until he had checked and rechecked his school work. Carson doesn't like to talk about this with other people, though. He has it under control. In fact, he doesn't really like to talk to other people at all because it's hard for him to look at other people's faces for a long time and then to figure out exactly what it is they expect him to say. Carson's parents thought he was an organizational genius who would breeze through high school and probably go to a highly competitive university. Then, one day, Mom noticed Carson's hands shaking as he rifled through his backpack while checking it before school. "What could be so frightening about eighth grade?" she wondered.

Perhaps you have noticed that one of your children exhibits a developmental picture that's a little different from your others. You may have wondered about an awkward gait, or difficulty maintaining eye contact. Are you worried that your child is fascinated by the larval stages of the banded hairstreak caterpillar while his peers are just happy to play with earthworms? You might have even asked your pediatrician about some of these apparently quirky behaviors, hoping to be reassured that everything was just fine. And, most likely, your pediatrician did just that.

"Don't worry about that, Mom. Sam or Samantha is just fine. Every child has a different developmental schedule." Then they give you that patronizing shoulder pat that makes you feel as though it's you that has the developmental delay. "There are many pathways within the acceptable norm, and it is never a good idea to compare one child with another. I never heard of a youngster who couldn't figure out how to tie his shoelaces before he got to high school." Your pediatrician smiles to reassure you while guiding you unmistakably toward the door. But you are not reassured.

Maybe you're a carpool parent who arrived early one day to pick up your child at nursery school. Aha! – the perfect opportunity to do some surreptitious observation from behind the dashboard. Was it just your imagination, or was everyone else's prodigy engaged in merry mudpile meetings, while yours stood aside discussing antique armature with the teacher? At your next parent conference, you ask about appropriate preschool development.

"You're worried about Kirby?" the teacher says in disbelief. "He's a little genius."

Sometimes the genius even makes it through elementary school with his or her academic reputation intact. He displays a remarkable rote memory and an incredible ability to retain and use arcane vocabulary. Her curiosity for intellectual pursuits, not really shared by the rank-and-file fourth grader outside of junior MENSA, encourages family members, teachers, and friends to consider clearing a shelf in the Hall of Brains for incoming talent.

School may not be too great an academic challenge in the early grades, though you can't help but notice that this child is clingier, more attached to home and family routine than others.

"Well," you tell yourself, "there's nothing wrong with that!" Part of you attributes the clinginess to the wonderful atmosphere you have created at home. Part of you questions your sanity.

Even with the benefit of besotted subjectivity, you can't help but notice that your child is a little clumsy ("So he won't be an athlete!"), anxious ("All the great thinkers obsess!"), and perhaps a little more distractible than teachers or counselors might prefer ("Well, she's thinking so far beyond her peers!"). Sometimes you wonder how your son can talk non-stop during a four-hour family trip, interrupted only by the urgent calls of nature. And to tell the truth, you yourself have to invent ways of zoning out as your daughter follows you around with seemingly endless information on her latest obscure interest. "I'm sure she'll grow out of that," you reassure yourself. "That child could have a conversation with a stone!" But as long as her classmates are still fascinated by these fourth-grade filibusters, you just assume your prodigy is headed for the Senate or at least for a career in daytime TV.

Unfortunately, when the little genius transitions from elementary to middle school, some of the characteristics that were remarkable to young admirers become much less important to prepubescent peers. Although Sarah could once entertain her classmates by reciting the entire developmental history of Barbie, the other sixth graders are beginning to notice that she asks too many questions, or talks too much, or doesn't really understand the subtler points of the suburban sartorial code.

Max could once mesmerize an audience of nine-year-old boys by describing details of powerful weaponry or by spouting Harry Potter scenarios verbatim. But in middle school, hormones supersede Harry. Since Max doesn't seem to understand the subtle cues in the all-important game of impressing girls, he is cast aside as his peer group begins the relentless pursuit of social success.

In addition to observing social and physical differences in development, you may be noticing that your allegedly brilliant child, the paragon of preschool, is also experiencing cognitive difficulties. He agonizes over homework assignments, and throws down his pencil and paper in frustration.

"I don't get it!" he screams, and slams the door to his room.

Perhaps your daughter is a perfectionist, spending six or seven hours a night on homework that you know should take no more than two. You hear her crying in her room as she rips up yet another sheet of paper and starts again on a perfectly pristine page. The child who can devour a 450-page volume and quote it virtually verbatim is rendered absolutely powerless by the assignment of a short written book report. What on earth is going on?

At this point, most concerned parents take their children to psychologists to see what is "bothering" them. They employ tutors to help with homework and teach children the "study skills" and "time management skills" which all learning specialists tout. They drag their offspring to the pediatrician for checkups, to the audiologist and ophthalmologist to see if there are any functional reasons for school problems. Finally, they throw up their hands in despair and wonder what to do next.

Although many practitioners assure parents that things will "simply improve with time," they usually do not. Even tutors, most of whom have a plethora of practices to remediate traditional language-based learning differences, are of little help. In fact, by the end of middle school, parents can be quite disturbed to realize that their youngster has few of the social or academic skills which characterize most representatives of the peer group. A parent can't help but worry about a child who returns from a day at school looking as though she has just served an entire tour of duty at the Hundred Years War. The daughter is frustrated because she has forgotten to turn in the homework she slaved over yesterday, doesn't really know what the homework assignment is for tomorrow, and has gotten into trouble for disobeying a rule she never understood in the first place.

In addition to ongoing generic anxiety about her daughter's fragile emotional wellbeing, Mom had to undergo a sudden religious conversion and whisper urgent prayers in the school parking lot because her daughter's visual-spatial skills are so poor that she walks carelessly in front of moving cars. Any parent who has ever suffered the rigors of parking lot pickup knows that this traffic zone is as deadly as a highway cloverleaf at rush hour. Even more disturbing, Hepzibah has no friends. Mom and Dad are losing friends themselves because no one seems to understand what is going on and people are beginning to lose patience.

"Send her to a good, strict boarding school with no boys," suggests the traditional father-in-law, jamming a monocle back on his recalcitrant eyeball. "That's what's distracting her. It's all hormones."

"Maybe she'd feel more comfortable at an experiential school on a Polynesian island?" offers Cousin Concepcion, the artist. "They don't worry about time, or clothes, and just let the sun and the sand steer their curriculum."

"They sent my brother-in-law's nephew to one of those *programs*," mentions the neighbor across the street. "After six weeks of hiking in the wilderness and eating cold lentils, he turned into an absolute angel."

When you have started to receive unsolicited advice from well-meaning individuals as diverse as shepherd to shaman, it is definitely time to seek professional assistance. You will never be able to help your child if you can't define what is going on. If you feel certain that you are seeing physical, behavioral, cognitive, and emotional symptoms that are different from those most children display, find a competent testing psychologist who can evaluate your child's basic cognitive and psychological competencies.

Unlike psychologists who choose to do therapy or experimental research, testing psychologists assess empirical and anecdotal information that they receive from children and family members to construct a picture of physical, emotional, behavioral, and cognitive development. But psychological assessment is only as good as the examiner who performs it. The testing psychologist must combine interpretive acumen with an ability to relate productively to your child and family. The outcome is inextricably tied to the information you give to the examiner and to the information produced by the psychometric measures administered. For these reasons, it is critical to be an informed consumer when finding the individual whose assessment could determine the course of your child's education or accommodations for the rest of a school career.

Sometimes, a psychologist will charge an initial consultation fee to meet the family and discuss the process. It is often well worth the fee to see if this practitioner is one who meets your expectations. In addition to seeing if personalities mesh, you should find out if the tests planned will give you information that could be useful in finding people who can provide productive interventions for your child, such as occupational therapists, reading comprehension specialists, speech and language pathologists, psychiatrists and psychopharmacologists, educational consultants, or perhaps therapists who specialize in helping children adjust to learning differences.

In most areas, the people most informed about nonverbal learning disorders work in hospitals with research centers or clinics with extensive child development services. There are also some private practitioners who understand the many ramifications, both subtle and overt, of this complex syndrome. In some cases, a local school system will offer to provide testing for free. The possibility of saving thousands of dollars is hard to resist. But remember that this is the same school system which fought for two years before agreeing to give your child a second set of books to keep at home.

What is the source of their sudden generosity? It is extremely important to evaluate not only the school system's ability, but also its agenda, before you entrust your child's brain to its scrutiny. All too often, true neurological needs are eclipsed by budgetary concerns. Assessments done in-house often recommend only the accommodations that the school is willing or able to provide. It can be worth investing in the services of an outside examiner in order to be sure that all findings are empirical and objective.

Although many parents will return to a store several times before they decide to purchase a sweater, examining every fiber and stitch, it is astonishing to note how many will get the name of a psychologist from a total stranger and book an appointment sight unseen. Although a hastily chosen sweater might severely impact your reputation for style or glamour, even the worst of worsted won't wreak the long-lasting havoc of a botched psychological assessment. Make sure that you use your sharpest consumer skills to protect your child when choosing the psychologist who will define his or her learning style to the outside world.

Don't be afraid to ask what type of training and experience the psychologist has had with nonverbal learning disabilities. Find out the ages of children most often seen in the practice. Trust your instincts. If you don't feel comfortable for any reason, move on to the next referral. The best results will occur when your family and the psychologist have a mutually respectful working relationship.

After you finally decide on a practitioner, remember that you deserve to receive a reasonable level of information and feedback throughout the process. At home, at school, and in all health-related encounters, you are your child's representative and advocate. You have not only the right, but the absolute need, to know the name and purpose of each test being administered. Unless the testing has been authorized by a school system or other outside institution, you also have the right to control who has access to this confidential information.

For most children, the first level of testing involves engaging a psychologist, educational psychologist, or school psychologist to administer a battery of psychoeducational tests. These tests are designed to assess your child's cognitive potential, the way your child processes information, and the current level of educational achievement. Your child's cognitive potential, or intelligence quotient (IQ), is not a measure of what has already been learned, but actually a measure of how your child can apply basic knowledge of the world around him to life.

The measures of processing information and the measures of educational achievement compare your child to normative peer standards. Depending on your child's age, ability to concentrate, and other characteristics which might affect testing, these measures are usually administered over a period of six to eight hours. In most cases, the testing is spread out over two or three sessions to prevent fatigue – not only for your child, but for the tester as well!

It is important for you to trust the testing psychologist you have chosen, and to believe that the testing protocol will include an assortment of measures that will provide a clear picture of your child's learning style. Although you do not need to understand the tests on a professional level, it is nice to know what each measure assesses and what the results indicate about your child. There are many resources in reference libraries and on the internet which will give you a preliminary understanding of the basic tests used in a psychoeducational evaluation. Some of the assessments commonly used are:

- *WISC – Wechsler Intelligence Scale for Children* (for kids under 16), or

- *WAIS – Wechsler Adult Intelligence Scale* (16 and over) – both assessments measure general intelligence in Verbal and Performance domains. If there is a large discrepancy between the two domains, it is sometimes not possible to calculate a valid full-scale IQ.

- *The Woodcock-Johnson Psycho-Educational Battery* – this series of tests measures your child's abilities against normative standards. The W-J assesses reading, writing, spelling, math, and other age-appropriate subjects.

- *The Wechsler Memory Scale or Children's Memory Scale* – this measure assesses the ability to recall and retain auditory, visual, and motor information.

- *The Brown ADD Scales* – this measure is used to assess levels of attention deficit. Because NLD is often confused with attention deficit/hyperactivity disorder (AD/HD) it is important to ascertain if such deficits originate from true AD/HD or from NLD.

- *The Rey Complex Figure Test and Recognition Trial (RCFT)* – this test measures visuospatial construction ability, immediate and delayed recall of visuospatial information, and recognition memory. Unless your testing psychologist has had a great deal of experience and training with this measure, it is often a good idea to have the RCFT administered by a neuropsychologist.

At times, the results of such preliminary testing indicate that there are discrepancies between your child's capabilities and accomplishments, between your child's documented results and peer norms, or even between disparate parts of your child's own brain. This last difference, known as intra-hemispheric dissonance, is one of the signals that alert us to the possible existence of NLD. It should also alert you to the fact that this is exactly the time to take your child to a pediatric neuropsychologist. The suggestion to see a neuropsychologist is not a cause for alarm. It is simply another step in the quest for obtaining the most detailed and specific information before embarking on a course of productive intervention.

A neuropsychologist is a professional trained at the graduate level to administer measures which assess how the brain receives, analyzes, organizes, and stores information obtained from the outside world. A careful interpretation of these assessments reveals how the individual constructs systems which program and regulate the conscious activity that leads to planning and goal fulfillment. By comparing a child's scores to a normative assessment, the neuropsychologist can give a family some idea of how a score is likely to reflect which of their child's abilities are intact and which are impaired.

It is important to remember that the function of the neuropsychologist goes well beyond the mere administration of in-office testing. Like all professionals who work with your child, a good neuropsychologist should analyze information obtained from records and previous testing, and should interview family members and professionals involved with the child's education and development. Drawing on information learned from what has been done before, the neuropsychologist will choose the appropriate test instruments, assess performance qualitatively and quantitatively, and make comparisons both across and within cognitive domains.

Before you choose the practitioner who will perform this complicated type of testing and feedback with your child and family, it is completely appropriate to ask some questions about professional training and range of experience. Just like other professionals in helping fields, neuropsychologists can specialize in a wide range of specific areas, and some may not have the right experience to be helpful to your child. For example, someone who specializes in geriatric neuropsychology or the neuropsychology of chronic diseases may not have the expertise you seek. It is always appropriate to ask for references from the medical or psychological community or to speak with former or current patients.

Once you have chosen a neuropsychologist with whom you feel comfortable, your family will be asked to submit a complete history of your child's cognitive, behavioral and social development. The neuropsychologist will then perform a series of empirical and observational tests to help determine the exact relationship between the messages your child's brain is broadcasting and the behaviors your child is displaying.

Before you go for testing, you should think back through your child's developmental history. Compare this child to siblings, as well as to the children of in-laws, cousins, neighbors, and friends. Bring up little things that might have been concerns you previously pushed aside for fear of being neurotic. For example, if you noticed that, all through nursery school, your child shied away from building toys and used Lego time to chat with the teachers, mention that. Trouble learning to tie shoelaces or learning to ride a bicycle may give the examiner important information that supports the clinical picture of fine and gross motor skills.

Think about the way your child uses the five senses and how he or she responds to sensory stimuli in the environment. If your child has a distinct preference for certain textures of clothing, will only eat foods that are bland and smooth, and complains about fluorescent lighting or other background light and sound, he or she may be experiencing a common companion of NLD, sensory integration dysfunction. Sometimes the brain is kind enough to contain its disorder in one domain, but that is rare indeed.

The synergy that powers all biological function means that when one area is affected, another makes adjustments to compensate. So NLD, though technically labeled a learning disability, essentially invades almost all domains of life. Behaviors that you thought were willful, manipulative, or obnoxious can be simply the results of your child's idiosyncratic response to specific stimuli. A mild tomato sauce that you think is sweet and bland may taste bitter or unbearably spicy to the child with sensory dysfunction. These responses are real, not just designed to make you prepare separate meals for a picky eater. Sharing information about your child's responses in school as well as out of school will help the neuropsychologist develop a comprehensive picture.

It stands to reason that you will discuss the transition from elementary to middle school, especially if it was more traumatic than you expected, but don't forget to specify other occurrences that you thought were particularly unusual or atypical. If there were more than a few isolated occasions when your child came home in tears complaining that no one liked him or her, remember to bring this up. Don't hide the painful conversation with the Brownie leader or Boy Scout den parent who said that your child just couldn't "get with the program." You are not hurting your child by recounting this diatribe of distress. Rather, you are helping to document a history of assets and deficits which will ultimately form the foundation for an active plan of intervention and support.

After taking a complete history, the neuropsychologist will see your child alone for a series of cognitive and functional tests. The instruments used for neuropsychological assessment will vary according to the issues documented by the history, previous psychoeducational assessments, and the neuropsychologist's initial observations. A thorough neuropsychological examination for a child suspected of having NLD should assess motor dexterity, tactual performance, sustained attention and concentration, processing speed and mental control, visual, motor integration, receptive, expressive, and pragmatic language, verbal, visual, and facial memory, visual problem-solving, and concept formation. Although there are a number of measures which can be used to arrive at this clinical picture, some of the more commonly used include:

- *California Verbal Learning Test* – assesses verbal learning and memory in older adolescents.

- *Lafayette Pegboard* – assesses motor dexterity.

- *Perdue Pegboard* – assesses motor dexterity.

- *Continuous Performance Test* – assesses attentional skills.

- *Trail Making Test* – assesses motor speed and attention functions.

- *Rey Complex Figure* – assesses visual memory.

- *Token Test* – assesses verbal comprehension of commands of increasing complexity.

- *Confrontation Naming Test* – assesses pragmatics and can indicate hemispheric dominance.

- *Wisconsin Card Sorting Test* – assesses executive processing.

- *Tactual Performance Test* – assesses tactual sensitivity and integration, including the ability to visualize spatial information.

- *Thematic Apperception Test* – assesses an individual's perception of interpersonal relationships.

- *WRAML Facial Memory* – assesses memory, the ability to learn, and examines verbal and language information separately from visual information.

- *Test of Language Competence* (selected subjects may be chosen) – assesses pragmatic language skills.

Don't try to second-guess your neuropsychologist. If you worry that not all domains are being assessed, ask respectfully why some tests that are regularly used seem to be missing from your child's protocol. If you are not satisfied with the answer, seek a second opinion. Do not disrespect your practitioner's professional expertise by trying to dictate what assessment measures should be used.

Once you have the results of psychoeducational testing and a neuropsychological assessment, you have a great deal of information about your child's capabilities, potential, assets, and deficits. For most children, this testing gives enough information to be used as the basis for accommodations and intervention. But on some occasions, there is still more information needed to complete the picture before a full understanding can be reached. Some children have been so affected emotionally by their learning differences that their state of mind alters their capability to perform. For others, their emotional status is the driving force behind their learning problems. In order to determine the balance of behavioral and emotional input, it can be helpful to have a psychologist administer personality testing, projective testing, and measures of anxiety and depression.

Tests which attempt to measure a person's basic personality style are very useful in determining clinical diagnoses. Often a pre-existing condition, such as obsessive compulsive disorder (OCD), can coexist with or masquerade as a learning disability. Some measures, like the MMPI (Minnesota Multiphasic Personality Inventory), are scored objectively, comparing several hundred "yes" or "no" answers to those of a normative population, assuming such a thing can be found. Others, like the well-known Rorschach "inkblot test," are much more subjective, leaving the examiner to interpret descriptions of the images and feelings your child experiences while looking at the blots.

Clinical measures, which assess depression and anxiety, like the Children's Depression Inventory (CDI) or the State-Trait Anxiety Inventory for Children (STAIC), can also give important information about the level of stress or emotional availability under which your child is functioning. Since most tests currently available for clinical use have a high standard of reliability and validity, their outcomes are generally accepted by people who perniciously question the "soft" diagnoses presented in psychoeducational reports.

Another category of information which may be necessary to complete the diagnostic picture can be supplied by a pediatric neurologist. If there is the possibility that a neurologic condition is the source of learning or behavioral issues, a neurological examination will identify the focal point and help to determine appropriate medical interventions.

Occasionally, results of testing will indicate that it is necessary to ask a specialist in a particular field to examine results that might be puzzling and to do more testing to gain further understanding. In these cases, you might be asked to have a speech and language professional test your child, or to have an occupational therapist do a complete workup for disorders of sensory integration and other issues that might be affecting optimal performance.

For some people and some conditions, the waiting and wondering ends when all the assessment information is complete. For NLDers and their families, however, getting the diagnosis marks the beginning of a lifetime's struggle to adjust to life from a slightly unusual perspective. Since the diagnostic category for NLD has not been clearly defined by medical professionals who define such syndromes in the *Diagnostic and Statistical Manual of*

Mental Disorders (DSM), or its European counterpart, *The International Statistical Classification of Diseases and Related Health Problems* (ICD), people making the diagnosis often disagree on which symptoms to include. To complicate matters, no two people with NLD are affected in the same way. Although there is a general categorical resemblance, each person with NLD, like a snowflake, is unique.

Most practitioners, however, agree on the characteristics originally defined by Dr. Byron Rourke, who first described the syndrome as a sub-category of learning-disabled students (Rourke 1989). Rourke believes that in order to qualify for the actual diagnosis, an individual must show a pattern of primary neuropsychological deficits in tactile perception, visual perception, and motor coordination which create secondary deficits affecting the way children pay attention to and explore their environment. The secondary deficits engender tertiary deficits in nonverbal memory, abstract reasoning, executive functions, and specific aspects of speech and language. This cascade of deficits ultimately creates varying but measurable levels of impairment in academic performance, social functioning, and emotional wellbeing.

Interestingly, NLD is defined not only by its deficits, but also by the presence of a number of assets as well. In order to meet the diagnostic criteria, individuals must display relatively intact simple motor skills, good auditory perception and attention, and rote memory for simple verbal material (Rourke 1995). Many individuals with NLD display relative strengths in receptive language and verbal expression. In fact, it is often the presence of the assets that make the diagnosis so complicated, since people with NLD often use their assets to compensate for their deficits until the material becomes too overwhelming to disguise.

But NLD, a quirky disorder if ever there was one, can actually get worse over time if no measures are taken to remediate the deficits. For this reason, it is critically important to get an accurate diagnosis and begin intervention as early as possible. In fact, the earlier the intervention, the better the prognosis. Although the label itself may offer neither solace nor support, starting to practice social skills, facial recognition, organization, or decoding nonverbal messages at an early age may minimize the impact of the deficit as your child matures. It can also be helpful to find teachers and mentors who understand that your child is neither disobedient nor disrespectful.

You've always suspected that this child is experiencing life in ways that are different and perplexing. Help defuse the confusion by teaching your child to understand the sensory and cognitive messages he or she is receiving. Make sure your child understands that NLD is not better or worse, but simply a different way of decoding the messages we receive all day, every day, from the world we live in. Henry David Thoreau put it best in *Walden*:

> If a man does not keep pace with his companions, perhaps it is because he hears a different drummer. Let him step to the music which he hears, however measured or far away.

> *(Thoreau 1969, p.565)*

Key points

1.   Observe your child's behavior carefully. If you believe your child's development differs from that of most peers, discuss specific concerns with your pediatrician. Make plans for a psychoeducational evaluation if you believe that your child is unhappy, frustrated, or challenged.

2.   If the original testing indicates areas of concern, follow through until all areas of psychological, neuropsychological, and neurological testing have been completed. Make sure that you understand the full developmental picture and prognosis when all testing has been completed. Ask the professionals who have tested your child to recommend reading materials which can help you understand your youngster's assets and deficits.

3.   Maintain a steady dialogue with teachers and caregivers. Make sure that everyone who interacts with your child is aware of strengths, weaknesses, and important personality characteristics.

4.   Stock up on patience, optimism, and unconditional love. These are the ingredients which will help bring your child to a life of happiness, productivity, and independence.

Chapter Two

Assets and Deficits

NLD has a set of very unusual diagnostic criteria. Even if an individual displays all of the neuropsychological deficits, at primary, secondary, and even tertiary levels, a positive diagnosis cannot always be made. In fact, no diagnosis can be based on impaired development unless the assets are as prominent as the deficits. It is no surprise that people, from professionals to parents, have trouble understanding the components of this complex syndrome. At times we are looking at children who exhibit unusual talents, and at other times, the same children seem to display severe developmental delays.

Paradoxically, the gifts that are given to people with NLD can at times be their worst antagonists. People don't expect children with fluent and copious verbal output to develop problems with language pragmatics and prosody. When these difficulties surface, children with NLD are often accused of being lazy or oppositional. Those of us who know them realize that nothing could be farther from the truth.

Similarly, the difficulties that children with NLD face in tasks that require visuospatial and organizational skills are often not understood. To most people, it seems almost inconceivable that a student who can read,

write, and speak convincingly would be unable to identify and recognize faces, expressions, gestures, or other nonverbal cues which are critical for appropriate communication and interaction.

An insightful adult with NLD (Flom 2002) once discussed his disability in light of this paradox:

> To me, one of the hardest parts of being NLD is that people don't GET IT. Although I have a large vocabulary, am great at trivia, and can solve difficult math problems, I still can't whistle, snap my fingers, or light a match. If a person is, say, dyslexic, then everyone knows that person has trouble reading. But if you tell people you are LD but good at reading and math they say, "If you're intelligent, then you're not learning disabled." And if you tell people that you can't read body language, they still get mad at you when you don't.

From the earliest works of Johnson and Myklebust (1967) and Rourke (1989) to the most current examinations of this elusive syndrome, most research agrees on the functional and behavioral categories in which people with NLD are likely to display assets and deficits. Children with NLD are generally expected to present the academic and behavioral profile shown in Table 2.1.

Table 2.1 NLD – Possible Assets and Deficits

Good at	Bad at
Rote memory	Holistic awareness
Attention to detail	Abstract math
Vocabulary and verbal ability	Nonverbal communication
Auditory retention	Social judgment
Early reading	Organization
Spelling skills	Transitions
Gross motor skills	Coordination

Such lists can be confusing and almost misleading. Many children who have been appropriately diagnosed do fit this general pattern, but there are many others with NLD who are atypical. Some are gifted mathematicians, others have fairly intact social skills, and some are astonishingly agile athletes.

Since no two people are affected in the same way, there is no prototypical model of a child or adult with NLD.

There is general consensus that the operational capacities affected by NLD are motor, visual-spatial, organizational, and social; but an individual with NLD can be affected in varying degrees in any category. This lack of recognizable unanimity has unfortunately delayed universal recognition of the syndrome. Nevertheless, anyone who takes the time to understand not only a person's behaviors and achievements, but also the neurological idiosyncrasies which impel them, can recognize a pattern of commonality in the general assets and deficits of people with NLD.

Neurologists who study the brain have proven through experiments and biomedical procedures, such as functional Magnetic Resonance Imaging (fMRI) and Single Photon-Emission Computed Tomograph (SPECT) scans, that the two sides of the brain are responsible for different activities. Many also believe that each hemisphere is responsible for a different way of thinking and processing information. Scientists who believe in left brain–right brain orientation use a table similar to Table 2.2 to illustrate how left brain thinkers differ from right brain thinkers.

Table 2.2 Characteristics of the Left and Right Hemispheres

Left brain thinkers	Right brain thinkers
Logical	Intuitive
Sequential	Random
Rational	Holistic
Analytical	Synthesizing
Objective	Subjective
Look at parts	Look at wholes

When we compare these characteristics to the assets and deficits of individuals with NLD, it seems apparent that people with NLD are similar to left brain thinkers. There are excellent qualities which are governed by the left brain, but they tend to be difficult to use successfully in the world without the right brain qualities that balance and integrate them.

Applied alone, the qualities of one side or the other produce a condition called intra-hemispheric dissonance – a situation in which the hemispheres of the brain conflict with each other rather than cooperate. So, while it may be wonderful to have a critical eye for details, it may not be useful to remember the minutiae characterizing every discrete component if you cannot understand how they come together as a whole. Similarly, logic is a prized quality in many circles, but it can be dry, dull, and ineffective when applied without intuition and creativity.

For this reason, effective accommodations for children with NLD should be based on efforts to maximize their assets and minimize their deficits. Essentially, this is what all of us do as we expose our talents and troubles to the world every day of our lives. In the case of people with NLD, however, the frustrations and failures can be so ingrained that deficits cannot begin to diminish without unequivocal intervention. Parents of children with NLD need to help professionals, educators, and caregivers understand the range of problems associated with the syndrome on emotional, behavioral, academic, and pragmatic levels. Although NLD fits the criteria for a learning disability since it affects the way in which people process information, the many categories affected by this diagnosis would better be served if it were called a *living disability*.

Sensory/motor assets and deficits

NLD affects sensory motor capabilities in a variety of ways. Some children with NLD suffer from a condition called hypotonia, which means that they have weak or floppy muscles. This can predispose them to tire easily and to have trouble standing for long periods of time. Fortunately, this effect of NLD has proven to be remarkably responsive to occupational therapy interventions. For example, sensory integration treatments that bombard a muscle with stimuli can dramatically improve the brain's ability to respond. A serious, long-term commitment to interventions like therapeutic sensory bombardment can ultimately create changes in perception that, in turn, promote increased efficiency along the neural pathways.

Another early motor difference in babies who are later diagnosed with NLD is their tendency to engage in sedentary rather than exploratory behaviors. In an interesting pattern which many of them use for the rest of their lives, these babies discover a system for getting what they need with the least expenditure of time and energy. Most children with NLD are hard-wired to distrust and avoid novelty. Additionally, since their auditory channels usually develop much more quickly than psychomotor skills, these children sit and point at items which interest them rather than initiate an exploration into the unknown. They will wait for a caregiver to bring it closer and explain what it is while they make an examination from a safe distance. By an uncannily early age, most babies with NLD learn that this method conserves the expenditure of energy they would need to crawl over to the object itself while simultaneously preventing encounters with unknown objects. Some children with NLD also struggle with oral-motor praxis. This may cause slurred speech or involuntary drooling, both of which can create social and emotional difficulties.

Some of the other motor deficits related to NLD can affect coordination, causing clumsiness, poor balance, and even disturbances related to academic output, such as graphomotor difficulty. Many NLDers have a tendency to fall, exposing themselves not only to a plethora of bruises but also to a resultant cascade of fears related to certain activities and, of course, taunting and bullying by schoolmates whose coordination skills appear streamlined and seamless. Problems with fine motor coordination as applied to multistep tasks are so characteristic of this syndrome that discovering if a child had trouble learning to tie shoelaces has almost become an informal diagnostic marker of NLD. Learning to ride a bicycle without training wheels is also in the category affected by this multisystem learning difference.

Byron Rourke explains that one of the primary strengths of children with NLD – the dominance of the auditory over the visual modality for processing information – is actually what predisposes them to some of the motor difficulties, since they prefer to hear about the environment rather than see or touch it (Rourke 1989). Sometimes, this lack of practice of physical activity combines with sensory dysfunction and other misinterpreted messages from the brain to cause general clumsiness, a distorted awareness of where the body begins and ends, an awkward gait, and other motor disturbances. Ironically, as is always true with this perplexing syndrome, the strong desire to overcome an obstacle for a particular reason can help a child with NLD conquer almost any deficit, even if it is neurologically based. This desire, the spark of stardom, is the characteristic that families must learn to encourage and validate in children with NLD.

Visual-spatial deficits

The rather misleading name of this syndrome – nonverbal learning disorder – refers primarily to the fact that visual-spatial deficits make it difficult for affected people to decode nonverbal signs, such as recognizing faces, understanding expressions that indicate certain feelings or emotions, and reading commonly used cultural signals used to communicate specific messages. It is this particular group of deficits – the visual-spatial organizational cluster – which prompts observers to describe some people with NLD as looking "clueless" or "like a deer in the headlights" when they are thrust into unfamiliar situations. The NLDer's difficulty in transforming visual-spatial information into activity creates a delay in response time which is neither typical nor tolerated in modern society.

Social deficits

The most important thing to remember about people with NLD is that each affected individual has a different personality. Some are inherently grumpy, cantankerous, and unyielding, while others are gentle, optimistic, and astonishingly resilient. Although the syndrome is generally associated with rigidity and inflexibility, these characteristics describe the cognitive processing and not the overall nature of those affected. While it is true that a steady diet of frustration and failure can turn even the sunniest disposition into a threatening storm, most individuals with NLD respond to people who understand their needs with appreciation and insight.

However, even if we dispel the myth of congenital crabbiness, the social disabilities that accompany this disorder can be painfully isolating and disheartening. Although affected at different levels, all people with NLD have trouble comprehending nonverbal communication. This includes not only facial expression, body language, and other gestures used for communication, but also tone of voice, nuance, and inference. As people with NLD begin to realize that certain situations can develop in ways they did not anticipate, they develop social anxiety and avoidance of novel situations. Many NLDers become very cautious as a result of these fears, but others, due to their inability to assess a situation exhaustively, blunder into totally inappropriate social territory. Since their social judgment is based on incomplete information, some NLDers are often uninformed of the inherent dangers or consequences of a situation.

Given the complexities and possibilities of their neurological assets and deficits, it is not surprising that NLDers often become overwhelmed. Some things make it through the brain maze directly and expeditiously. NLDers are known to be excellent students of history, vocabulary, and similar fact-based subjects. But once complex analysis is required, the systems which process cognitive information for NLDers tend to work in a way that seems labored and arduous. When this starts to happen in school, it is quite confusing for young NLDers. Often they start to avoid the subjects which cause difficulty. When it is no longer possible to avoid those subjects, some think of ways to avoid school.

Executive function disorder

In today's world of diagnostic chic, executive function disorder is definitely the trendy newcomer. But ironically, this dysfunction of the cognitive system's CEO is just another name for the intrinsic flaw affecting cognitive, motor, and social processing in people with NLD. In a large company, not unlike the human body, there are many different departments which perform discrete functions. However, ultimately, they must all be authorized by the CEO. If he or she does not fund and support a department, that department is simply not empowered to do its job. It either lies dormant until reactivated, or shuts down completely and is phased out of the business.

Sometimes closing a department is actually good for business. When a competent CEO of the brain makes decisions about closing an area that might impair optimal performance, it is called pruning. But when decision-making areas in the brain's frontal lobes are damaged or temporarily "out of the office," havoc ensues in the departments that rely on instructions from above to function. Similarly, in people with NLD, there is a breakdown of communication from the brain to the departments that perform certain tasks. This breakdown delays or even disables the completion of those activities. For example, many people with NLD suffer from difficulty with working memory, a "department" controlled by the brain's CEO.

Working memory enables people to retain information while using it to complete a task. It is a critical skill to have for continuing to the next step in a math problem after you have learned a concept or formula. When the CEO cuts funding to the department of working memory, it can be frustrating or impossible to carry out complex tasks such as those required in mathematics above the sixth-grade level.

Most people with NLD definitely manifest some of the problems associated with executive function disorder, although NLD as a syndrome is more pervasive than a disorder affecting only the frontal lobes. To put it more simply, we can assume that all people with NLD suffer some effects of executive function disorder, but not all people with executive function disorder have NLD.

Explosions and implosions

Although each person with NLD has his or her specific manner of showing frustration or disappointment, most manifestations fit into one of two categories – meltdown or shutdown. Ross Greene defines "meltdown" as the point when a child who is completely overwhelmed by frustration loses his capacity for coherent rational thought, describing children who have simply failed to develop adequate and age-appropriate flexibility and frustration tolerance. Although not all of the children Greene depicts in *The Explosive Child* have NLD, his description helps us understand the meltdown mechanism in children who do (Greene 1998).

Since meltdown behavior can adversely affect families, school, and peer relationships, as well as a child's own sense of self, Greene suggests approaching these difficulties proactively by teaching children to deal with frustration in an adaptive manner. As logical as it seems that teaching flexibility to an inflexible child will expand his parameters of function and comfort, such instruction may be the hardest task that the parent of a child with NLD can face. Nevertheless, flexibility is the single most important adaptive mechanism our children can learn in the attempt to make the world less confrontational. Still, some children with NLD, left with no alternatives for coping, rely on meltdown to inform the world that a situation is completely intolerable or that their sensory systems are completely overloaded. It is critically important to learn where, when, and why these extreme behaviors occur so that you can prevent circumstances from conspiring to disconcert your child again.

Perhaps even more insidious to the ultimate wellbeing of the child with NLD is the occurrence of shutdown. Instead of melting down in an active, vociferous manner, the child who internalizes emotions and feelings can disguise a great deal of frustration and despair before the intensity of his or her pain is apparent to others. Gradually, at a pace unique to each individual, a child or young adult with NLD may choose to dissociate from activities, discontinue attempts to keep up with schoolwork and homework assignments, and stop participating even in the few extracurricular pursuits which have been a source of pleasurable feedback and interaction. Usually, these children become less talkative and start spending more time alone in their rooms and away from family activities. They bear the classic signs of clinical depression, and some, in fact, respond well to psychopharmacological intervention intended to remediate that problem. However, in children with NLD, the symptoms that mimic neurobiological depression are most often the symptoms of reactive depression induced by their ongoing failure to meet social, academic, and personal goals.

Emotional shutdown occurs when overreactions put more stress on the nervous system than it can handle. For the child with NLD, who always has difficulty defining and expressing feelings, it is not a far leap from minimal sensation to emotional numbness. Once a child is paralyzed by such overwhelming numbness, it is extremely critical to re-engage and re-inspire that child with whatever resources are available, including medical and therapeutic interventions. If you find that school is the main source of the problem, it may not be too drastic to withdraw your student from school.

Remember that children with learning differences have a higher suicide rate than their neurotypical peers. Children and young adults with NLD, moreover, have the highest suicide rate of all. In light of the great confusion and frustration experienced when trying to live in a society where very few acknowledge their unusual perspective, this is a devastating but not a surprising finding. Working to recalculate that negative statistic will mean learning to identify the emotional states that precede full-blown shutdown and formulating the appropriate interventions to bring young NLDers back to active participation in the development of their own positive futures.

Key points

1. Each side of the brain has specific characteristics. Using both together produces symmetry and coordination. Using one hemisphere at a time causes a series of cognitive deficits and maladroit behaviors.

2. NLDers use cognitive processes that are lateral and literal.

3. Because NLDers are often exposed to strain, discomfort, and environmental annoyance, they seek sensory stimulation to gain cognitive, emotional, and sensorimotor equilibrium.

4. Many NLDers have a poor working memory, difficulty visualizing, and an inability to generalize. Without consistency, they must recreate their environment at great cognitive cost each day.

5. NLDers are threatened by their environment since they often lack control over the sensorimotor, visual-spatial, organizational, and social aspects of their lives. They become extremely anxious if they believe that their physical or emotional safety is at risk.

6. Meltdowns and shutdowns are the NLDer's way of begging for help in a world that has become overwhelming. They should be approached supportively, not punitively.

7. The most disabling aspects of the NLD syndrome are inflexibility and anxiety. These symptoms are actually two sides of one coin. NLDers are often so anxious about change that they become rigidly afraid to try something new. *Voilà!* – inflexibility.

Chapter Three

NLD-Friendly Environments at Home

While they are still struggling to understand themselves and their disability, many children with NLD face daily discomfort and defeat in the outside world. As their parents and the people who love them, we must strive to make home the place where they feel emotionally and physically safe. Although all children can benefit from such an environment, it is critically important for children with NLD to know that there is a place where they are understood, appreciated, and unconditionally loved. Soccer heroes might begin on the lawn, and basketball greats on a polished court, but NLD superstars evolve at home.

There are no architects, interior designers, or monthly journals that can help families who are looking for professional help on creating NLD-friendly homes. No matter how many waiting rooms you ransack, you will never find a copy of *Left-Brained Homes and Gardens* or *Architectural Digest for the Neurologically Impaired*. Homes that are friendly to children with NLD grow out of each child's unique set of assets, deficits, preferences, and pleasures. They reflect each family's taste, modified by experience, knowledge, training, awareness, and the desire to simplify the life of the NLDer they love. As I stress often, it is almost impossible for our NLDers to change the neurological configurations which impel them to approach the world as they do. Those of us who

are neurotypical, however, can foresee negative consequences and do our best to eliminate them before they occur.

The easiest accommodations to make for your NLDer are those which involve physical safety. Each NLDer has a different set of assets and deficits, but most face certain sensorimotor challenges which may affect navigation in confined spaces. As soon as your NLDer achieves independent mobility, you may have to make a decision about your collection of fragile Dresden ballerinas. Although most young NLDers are not inherently exploratory or inquisitive in a tactile sense about objects around them, some may have difficulty interpreting the brain's commands to the body. The arm that Hyperion intends to use for maintaining balance as he climbs the staircase may take an alternate pathway through the knick-knack shelf on its way to the balustrade. He will be more surprised than you to see the Dresden dancers do their final échappé.

Until you are sure that your child knows how to use kitchen tools and other household implements that might be inherently dangerous, make sure that everything is stored in places which are not readily accessible. Remember that NLDers often use impaired judgment when making decisions that could affect their own safety or the safety of others. Sue Thompson may have been the first to say "I shouldn't have to tell you" when speaking of NLDers (Thompson 1997), but she certainly will not be the last. Even when your NLDer claims that your instructions and restrictions are infantilizing, keep repeating them until you have tangible evidence that it is no longer necessary to do so. Unless your child is planning to become a surgeon, it is hard to be a superstar when she has cut her forefinger to the bone while attempting to slice a bagel.

When you have established what will make your children feel comfortable, arrange your homes to meet their needs without creating a fuss and without making announcements that call attention to their disabilities. You may indeed guarantee Peter's physical safety by ordering stable kitchen chairs that make it impossible to wobble in all directions, including some that have not even been identified as points on the compass. But physical safety will seem like an insignificant afterthought if you announce to the whole family that these chairs are Peter-proof – they do not tilt, nor bend, nor balance on one leg.

Since we are already in the kitchen, this is probably a good place to make decisions about food that will keep a range of people happy, from your NLDer to the family dentist, your favorite pediatrician and gastroenterologist and, most important, the local fire prevention brigade. The first rule for food is, of course, physical sustenance. Make sure that your child is eating the proper amount of whatever food groups are in fashion at the moment. We will discuss food and its foibles at length in Chapter 7, so it is enough here to point out that part of making your NLDers comfortable at home is teaching them to be independent enough to find healthy, interesting snacks and to prepare light meals as soon as it is age appropriate to deal with utensils, cans, microwaves, and the like. Be acutely aware of your child's specific assets and deficits before attempting any culinary escapades. Some NLDers, like many neurotypicals, should never attempt to prepare anything more complicated than a peanut butter and jelly sandwich.

Cooking is an activity which involves intangible talents that surpass sensorimotor skills. But those who are interested can learn to prepare things they enjoy and to return the kitchen to a reasonable facsimile of its former self after their accomplishments. Like all teaching with this unique segment of the population, the art of cooking requires time and patience in incalculable proportions. Once you have finished, though, you will have imparted another skill which travels well along the road to productivity, independence, and stardom.

When NLDers are very young, they will probably be safe if you baby-proof or child-proof your home according to the safety guidelines established for neurotypical children. Just make sure to take sensory issues into consideration as well. Some children with NLD absolutely cannot tolerate the buzz and brightness of fluorescent lighting or the interplay of figures and tone in brightly patterned wallpaper. For NLDers, sensory assaults of this nature should be considered issues of physical health because the resulting reactions can truly compromise their wellbeing. As your child grows and develops new competencies, continue to examine each room for a reassessment of the areas where you have made accommodations for physical and sensory safety.

Laying the foundation for a home built on emotional safety is a much more complex procedure than safeguarding physical security. Emotional safety is not as easy to measure or anticipate. Often it is recognizable only when it is gone. How then can we guarantee our NLDers this basic component of productivity and independence? The most efficient way is to consider your NLDer's unique needs as they relate to each area of your home. Evaluate the issues which affect your child and think of ways which can alleviate potential sources of distress or frustration. Some topics will be global, such as clarifying expectations and identifying parent/child roles, but others will be specific to a defined area and a particular child.

Although you may believe that you are intimately familiar with your child's needs, likes, and dislikes, make sure to ask questions from the embarrassingly fundamental to the highly complex before you try to reorganize or redecorate. Even when the changes you plan to implement are in the spirit of becoming NLD-friendly, make sure you have explored your child's interests and needs before proceeding.

When a child I know rather well reached the age of 13, his parents decided to honor his passage from childhood to adolescence by redecorating the room previously occupied by two older brothers. He was told that within several deviations from the norm of socially acceptable décor, he had free rein to choose new wallpaper, carpet, bed and bedding, furniture, and color scheme. The family hoped that by helping their son create a haven for maximum sensory serenity, he would enjoy a comfortable environment for living and learning throughout his teenage years.

Perhaps there is a reason that not many people with NLD pursue careers in interior design. First the son requested that the walls be painted black. His parents explained that paint was not an option due to the unevenness of previous layers of wallpaper. They then intimated that such dark surroundings would probably not be conducive to the years of productivity they hoped lay ahead of him in middle school and high school. Uncharacteristically agreeable, the budding designer agreed to look through books of wallpaper to find a suitable pattern.

He and his mother spent more time visiting wallpaper stores than most couples spend courting. Patiently, he turned page after page and vetoed pattern after pattern. His mother took him to every wallcovering emporium within commuting distance.

"Can I help you look?" she offered hopefully.

"No."

"Could you just give me a few guidelines so I could do some triage before you go through every book in the store?" (His mother was beginning to feel a chink in the armor of her patience.)

"No."

"Why don't you just describe some colors or patterns you like so I can look through some of the books while you look through others?"

The NLDer's mother had clearly taken leave of her senses. If he could describe imaginary wallpaper by color and design, he probably wouldn't have NLD. But he surprised her with his answer.

"Mom, just let me do it. I know exactly what I'm looking for."

Mom felt a tiny spark of hope flicker.

"You do?" she asked ingenuously. "Tell me about it! What *are* you looking for?"

The son gaped at his mother in disbelief, clearly expressing astonishment at her ignorance. As he maintained eye contact for much longer than was his habit, he stared mockingly, implying that she was an utter idiot for not knowing what should be so apparent. Finally he spoke.

"I'm looking for the same paper that was on the walls before."

The mother was well aware of her son's difficulty with transitions. She had worked out elaborate systems with teachers for introducing new subjects and new routines. Before vacations or schedule changes, she carefully discussed what would happen until it became expected and familiar. When her son grew out of favorite items of clothing or was forced to relinquish a beloved pair of shorts because the temperature was below freezing, she was careful to tread gently until he had weathered the transition. But she had never realized that changing wallpaper might be similarly traumatic for a child with NLD.

After questioning him about all the things that had made him comfortable in the old room and what he would need to be comfortable in the redecorated room, mother and son negotiated some compromises. The wallpaper pattern would remain the same, but instead of navy blue squares on a white background, the grid would be black on white, a pattern that Mom had seen at least 73 times in her paper perusals. Everything that had coordinated with navy and white would now be refreshed to coordinate with black and white.

Mother and son found a charcoal gray carpet which would cover a multitude of NLDisms. Furniture was painted black or white, bedspreads went from shades of blue to shades of black and gray, and extremely serviceable black sheets completed the décor. The son was mollified to have essentially the same room, albeit a few tones lower chromatically. The parents were happy to give their third son his own opportunity to destroy walls, carpet, furniture, and bedding. And what could be more ironically suited to an NLDer than a room of his own which was completely decorated in shades of black and white?

As we are located in the bedroom, this is a perfect opportunity to discuss two other issues of emotional safety for NLDers which revolve around this locale. The first issue is sleep or, for some NLDers, the lack of it. If you have taken the opportunity to observe your child's habits, you will see that he or she seems to have a rather unusual body clock. As we will learn in the chapter on hurrying (Chapter 10), NLDers do things at their own pace, in their own time. The same phenomenon generally applies to sleeping. As parents and caregivers, however, it is beneficial for us to help them adjust their body clocks to a sleeping/waking regimen which is attuned to the responsibilities of age-appropriate lifestyles.

Just as NLDers have difficulty with educational transitions and interior design transitions, they have difficulty with biophysiological transitions. When people transition from wakefulness to sleep, a number of physical and emotional functions must work in concert to facilitate the process. It is possible that NLDers have trouble coordinating these functions. Often they have trouble falling asleep. More often, they have trouble making the transition from sleep to wakefulness. Do not discount their problems in this area.

In your NLDer's bedroom, make sure that you have created the optimal environment for sleep. Be sure that the area around the bed is cool, quiet, dark, and comfortable. Many NLDers are more comfortable having their mattress on the floor, because they get better proprioceptive feedback. If they are bothered by external sights or sounds, consider using blackout curtains, eye shades, ear plugs, white noise machines, humidifiers, and other devices designed to facilitate sleep. Make sure that all pillows and bed linen are free of allergens or fabrics that make your NLDer uncomfortable. If you have tried all possible accommodations and are still unable to encourage a healthy sleep routine, consult your pediatrician or other specialist for help. It may even be necessary to refer your child or adolescent to a sleep clinic if the problem persists.

Although there are many young people who like to study at the kitchen or living room table, the majority of students retreat to the familiar comfort of their own desk, which is usually located in a dedicated corner of their own bedroom. This is the second issue of great concern facing the NLDer and the bedroom. It is important for you to help your NLDer develop a workspace where it will be comfortable to study and learn. Like everything else that we have discussed, this must be a cooperative effort between you and your NLDer.

Although you might assume you know what elements you child needs for effective work habits and organization, you will be surprised at what you will learn when you discuss what is really critical. Take notes and do the shopping together. If you believe that the task might be handled more effectively with the help of an impartial third party, hire a professional organizer or a specialist in creating effective learning spaces for students with special learning needs. But first, have a conversation with your child which touches upon some of the following categories:

1. *What part of the bedroom will be dedicated to the workspace?* Some children prefer to do their homework on their beds or on the floor. In that case, a rolling station or a portable desktop might be a good idea. Others are quite comfortable with more traditional desk-and-computer configurations. In that case, just decide on a place which can accommodate the amount of electric power that will be necessary, and invite the furniture delivery person right over. Many children with NLD, however, prefer to work in an area that offers minimal sensory stimulation rather than use a desk which is right out in the open. For them, consider placing the study area into a protected nook or even a closet. It may sound like cruel and unusual punishment, but if you buy a hanging clothes rack and move your child's wardrobe out, a closet with the door removed makes a great spot for a desk and some bookshelves. Whether or not your child will choose to come out of the closet is definitely material for a totally different chapter.

2. *Ambiance.* You may not get rated annually by the *International Workspace Review,* but you should help your children determine what type of environment produces their best work. After

attributing years of procrastination to dissatisfaction with my surroundings, I have discovered that I like to work where it's quiet, bright, and light. Most of my children prefer to have their scholarly efforts accompanied by deafening music. My husband darkens everything but the spot where he is reading or writing and listens to opera. Ask your children what they prefer. Some like the feeling of being around others, some like peace and quiet, and others enjoy background music. Some do best when there is chaotic din in the background; the additional stimulation actually allows them to focus in on their own work.

3. *Lighting.* The quality of lighting can make or break the attempt to study. Fluorescent lighting, as I have mentioned before, can be extremely uncomfortable for some people with sensory dysfunction. Others have preferences or dislikes for halogen, incandescent, or natural light. People are also responsive or defensive to the angle of the light and the direction from which it comes. If you don't ask, you'll never know.

4. *Temperature.* When I plant shrubs or bulbs, I always respect the instructions that come along from the nursery. "Needs bright sunlight or partial light." "Must plant four inches from next plant." "Prefers northern light." But as we already know, children don't come with instructions, and for children with NLD, most things are counterintuitive, anyway. Nevertheless, if you notice that your daughter likes to wear fleece footie pajamas when she studies and usually has three or four cats snuggling up on her lap, she probably won't enjoy working in an Arctic draft or under the air conditioning vent. Some people, ironically the polar opposites of those mentioned above, like to work in their unmentionables or even less. They feel freer when completely unencumbered, and might do very well near the warm sunny window, as long as it doesn't face right into a religious school. But generally most people, even NLDers, read best in a cool room so that they can wear something sensorily cozy and satisfying that doesn't interfere with what the brain is absorbing. For writing tasks, most people like to have their arms unrestricted.

5. *Changeability.* After you have gone to all the trouble of finding the ideal place for your NLDer's workstation, you may find that the best learning environment for your child is one that moves. If you are lucky, you will have a child who likes to move only every few weeks, but some like to move every couple of days or even every half hour. This can depend on what subject is being studied, or perhaps on the alignment of the planets. In other words, the preference is totally iconoclastic and quirky. Portable workstations with supplies hanging in baskets or rolling file charts work wonders for these moveable beasts.

6. *Organizing the supplies.* Sit with your child and make a list of the supplies he or she regularly uses. Then group like-things together. A simple system for organizing school and study materials is to group things in categories of:

    (a) things I write with

    (b) papers I like to keep handy

    (c) books I like to have near when I do my homework

    (d) things I have to write on tonight.

7. *Chairs.* Some like them soft, some like them hard, some like them bouncy. Now what were you thinking with your minds in the gutter? We're talking about chairs, one of the three most important things for accomplishing good work habits. I know you're wondering what the other two are – a desk, and a brain, of course! Anyway, a good chair for studying should have a height that is appropriate to the work surface. It is extremely difficult to do homework when your entire head is under the desk. When you are sitting on the chair, your feet should be able to rest firmly on the floor with knees at a 90 degree angle. If this makes it impossible for you to see anything other than the underside of the workspace, then let your dangling feet rest on a small footstool or box. Many children with sensorimotor issues enjoy sitting on a balance ball, which gives them good sensory feedback while working.

8.   *Desk.* The surface of the desk should be comfortable to use as a surface for writing. A highly polished texture like glass or shiny plastic may be distracting, so make sure your children can pay attention to their work before choosing a desktop which allows them to see their faces in leagues of little laminated lines. Some people prefer light worktops to dark. Others find it even easier to focus when they use a desk pad or blotter which limits and defines the work area. Ask your children if they prefer using a textbook holder so that they can see the book upright or if they prefer to have the reading plane and the writing plane at similar levels.

9.   *Tech center.* No modern study area would be complete without a full range of assistive technology and electronic support. Ask your child what equipment is absolutely critical or provide the equipment suggested by the assistive technology report from your occupational therapist or technology specialist. Your child will almost certainly need a computer. Laptops are generally preferred by young people today for their ease of portability. They are no longer bulky or overly expensive. Many students use an AlphaSmart, an integrative keypad from which they can download information to their computer when they come home from school. For children with graphomotor difficulties, the AlphaSmart is a helpful and portable instrument. Newer models are available with built-in personal organizers so that your children will never be unaware of daily schedules. Finally, for children with NLD, a printing calculator is a useful tool. Math assignments are much easier to complete when students can see the numbers lined up and legibly printed.

Despite the most carefully instituted plans, there will always be the children who acknowledge their super study space and prefer a prone position on the playroom floor. Others will agree that they have everything they could ever want, but feel lonely unless other family members are around while they work. Remember that you are not competing for the cover story in *Better Homes and Burdens*. Having your child do homework is the primary goal. The location is secondary.

Another site of many NLD moments, both fond and frenetic, is the bathroom. For many NLDers, the functions related to personal hygiene and care of the body seem to be complicated by sensory issues, hypotonia, and fine motor difficulties. If we look at the comprehensive categories affected by this syndrome – motoric, visual-spatial, organizational, sensory, and even social – we can generate an alarmingly extensive list of functions which includes lack of coordination, balance problems, poor visual recall, faulty spatial perceptions, problems with spatial relations, difficulties adjusting to transitions, deficits in social judgment, and sensitivity in any of the sensory modes, including visual, auditory, tactile, taste, or olfactory. Add to this the deficits in executive function that NLDers are known to have, and our list grows to include neuropsychological functions which might apply to this site such as decision-making, planning, initiative, assigning priority, sequencing, problem-solving, impulse control, establishing goals, monitoring results of action, and self-correcting.

When I think of the disasters that might result from the unfortunate interaction of the medicine cabinet and an NLDer, I wonder if it might be appropriate to retain an armed guard for the bathroom. My imagination is no more sanguine as it leaps to the toilet or bathtub. Nevertheless, you have a non-negotiable responsibility to imbue your NLDer with the social cognitive age-appropriate skills related to any room found in your home or in any dwelling in what we all generally consider to be the civilized world.

The first of all non-negotiable activities related to the bathroom is, of course, toilet training. If you can't seem to get the message across by whatever age is considered appropriate in your social community, let me suggest that you contact one of the many professionals who can help you help your child. Remember, however, that, with toileting, just as with any activity that your child attempts, all learning takes place against the backdrop of the NLD pattern of assets and deficits. The following guidelines may make the bathroom more NLD-friendly as you approach the Herculean task of helping your child understand the benefits of pants over Pampers.

NLDers, as a rule, do not have the same drive toward reciprocal social relationships as their neurotypical peers. For this reason, they may not be interested in achieving the milestone of wearing big boy or big girl pants to impress their parents or an older sibling. After you regale them with the tantalizing tale of Tarquin's terrific toileting or Ursula's unflappable undies, most typical NLDers, if indeed such types exist, would probably reply, "So what's your point?"

Children with executive function disorder may find it challenging to learn the organizational and sequential information involved with toileting. The sequence of sensorimotor functions involved in toilet training may be overwhelming for NLDers even though it is not a particularly difficult task for their neurotypical age mates. In addition, NLDers may not have the motivation to transition from a diaper, which has served quite well for two, three, four years (or, heaven forfend, even longer), to the intrinsically more difficult system of toileting.

The bathroom environment usually includes bright lights, loud flushing noises, confusing tactile experiences related to removing clothing and dressing again, smelly soaps, and rushing hot or cold water. It is not a place where most young NLDers would choose to spend much time. And for some young children affected with sensory dysfunction, the notion of sitting on a chair with a big hole right over water can be very disquieting. For these reasons, many NLDers, who use logical left brain solutions from a very early age, may conclude that being toilet trained is less of a benefit than generally described.

So, even though it may seem as though your NLDers are taking an awfully long time to train relative to their peers, this may be one area where it doesn't hurt to "pamper" them a bit. I have had the privilege of meeting many adults with NLD. To the best of my knowledge, not one of them is still in diapers.

Having established that it is impossible, and, in fact, unconscionable, to eliminate all problems related to the bathroom, let us also remember that it is equally impossible to eliminate all problems related to elimination. Some NLDers have problems with toilet training because they are hyposensitive to the signals most people recognize as an early warning that urination or defecation is imminent. Some learn to be dry during the day because when awake they can be alert to the signals, but experience enuresis through pre-adolescence because the signals at night are not strong enough to wake them from a deep sleep.

Even more noisome is the cohort that struggles with encopresis, the inability to control bowel movements. Although most psychiatrists or child psychologists will tell you that encopresis is a symptom of severe anger or rage, in NLDers it can simply be a combination of hypotonia and low sensory awareness. It is important to help your NLDer understand what is happening so that he or she won't develop stomach pains or food avoidance problems in an attempt to have more control over elimination.

Kids with NLD who have regressions in toilet training, including accidents, and even recurring enuresis and/or encopresis, naturally find these problems embarrassing and difficult to deal with. It is incumbent upon parents to be a child's best advocate by treating this as a no-guilt situation in a matter-of-fact manner. Place no blame. Get the best help you can. Time, patience, maturation, and an unusually large supply of sheets will help you and your NLDer get through this indelicate issue until it finally resolves.

As we have mentioned earlier, habits that look like hygiene from hell are often simple manifestations of sensory incompatibility. If your NLDer's toothbrush has been observed writing letters to Miss Lonelyhearts, ask why he isn't brushing. If you suspect that the last spool of dental floss you purchased might win a Ripley's Commendation for Length, perhaps you should ask your child if there is truly an interminable amount available or if it is simply not being used. The shampoo guaranteed to make Susie's hair shinier than sunlight will probably never work if it remains in the bottle. Discuss your child's bathroom rituals at age-appropriate levels to determine exactly what is happening. A gentle conversation in a nonjudgmental tone can help alleviate problems that range from lactose intolerance to slimy conditioner.

When you know that your child has mastered certain skills but still refuses to perform them, find whatever euphemism makes you comfortable with the word "bribe" and devise a system of small rewards for your child's compliance with whatever activities you consider non-negotiable. Make a list which details everything your child must do in the morning and in the evening. Go over the list at a set time every day, and give your NLDer the opportunity to make up for things that somehow slipped through. It helps if a person your child admires can create the list. Hero worship is a much more positive social behavior than bribery.

An NLDer I know rather well seemed to be suffering either from color blindness or the belief that green was a more resplendent representation for teeth than white. After retiring his toothbrush, his formerly magnificent mouth began to resemble a toothpaste ad for the Incredible Hulk. His sister, a devotee of determined dentistry, approached her mother worriedly.

"Mom, his teeth are green. Eeeeuww, it's so gross. Wait until Dr. Santiago sees him."

Strangely, the second eldest brother had a different opinion.

"Hey, Ma, did you see his teeth? They are totally green. That is *so* cool!"

The oldest, already an adolescent, knew best of all.

"I can't believe you allow him to walk around with teeth like that. What kind of parent are you? Do you have any idea what types of bacteria he could be exposed to?"

The mother acquiesced. She said to the oldest child, "You really are right. I don't know how I could have been so lax. Could you help me? I'd like to make a list of hygiene activities for him to accomplish every morning and every evening. If I do it, though, he'll probably think I'm nagging. If it came from you, it might work better."

The oldest child gave her a look only adolescents can produce. It seamlessly blends pity with contempt.

"All right, I'll do it. But don't forget this when I need something."

"Oh no," thought the mother. "I'm not likely to forget."

The next morning, the following sign was taped to the mirror in the children's bathroom:

A.M. and P.M.

Yo, Snaggletooth! Do it and don't ask why.

1. Squeeze toothpaste out on your toothbrush.
2. Brush for two minutes – top and bottom – I'm watching.
3. Wash brush and return to holder.
4. Wash face and hands. (Yes, with soap.)
5. Dry with towel.

Big Brother is really, really watching you, Pusmouth.

The mother, once a literature major, was not a great fan of the syntax or the language. But she had to admit that the method worked. The youngest son's teeth reversed from emerald to ivory. Mission accomplished.

Perhaps even more basic than dental health, and somewhat larger in scale for most beings of normal proportion, is the issue of showering and bathing. From an early age, NLDers develop sensitivities to certain types of soaps, shampoos, washcloths, and towels. Some can even distinguish between hard and soft water and complain that they cannot tolerate one or the other. When your NLDer complains of a sensory issue, it is a completely real and valid complaint. A shampoo that might seem pleasantly fragrant to you can seem noxiously malodorous to a hypersensitive olfactory system. Your NLDer's reactions are not manipulative or selective. They are uncontrollable neurological responses.

Although it is definitely one of your non-negotiable duties to find the products which will make your child comfortable enough to learn to bathe independently, there will be some days when there will be no cells available for teaching or learning. If your children are young enough, give them a quickie sponge bath or shower, dry them, dress them, and tuck them in. Save the messages for days when there are receptors available to pick them up. By the way, the ten-minute sponge bath/towel-dry-tuck-in generally stops being appropriate by the time you have to stand on a ladder to towel-dry your son's hair.

When your children are older, and it is clear that they should be washing independently, you can only hope that they will not be cited by the Board of Health for appearing in public without having showered. One day without "I shouldn't have to tell you" will probably not delete any serious life lessons that have already been learned. In fact, you might even find an opportunity for praise. "You did an amazing job today. Why don't you just jump into bed and shower in the morning?"

Remember that everything we can reinforce with credible, appropriate praise is much more likely to be remembered as a positive family experience. And that's really what building an NLD-friendly home is all about. Our kids need to know that when things get hard, there's someone to acknowledge that they are trying their best, that they are loved, and that when they need help, there is someone who cares enough to give it. This is a message that we can't offer too frequently. Sometimes it seems as though our kids don't understand it, but that's never true. They may not know how to acknowledge it, but it's the most important message they can hear.

There are two areas left where you must take extra care to make sure that your home is NLD-friendly. One is actually not inside your home at all, but in your yard and neighborhood. On your own property, make sure that all athletic equipment is safe, fun, and non-threatening for your child. If you have a pool or tennis court, be sure that your child knows basic safety rules and also develops at least minimal competencies. Don't force children to live in places where their own back yards highlight their deficits.

It's much more difficult to insure that your neighborhood is NLD friendly. For some children with social cognitive deficits, it is almost impossible to be a "regular" kid beyond the confines of their own bedrooms. The degree to which your child will be accepted depends on the personalities of children dominating the social scene combined with the outward vulnerability of your child. Don't underestimate the power of children. They are champions at survival of the fittest. Although some seem to have an innate sense of compassion from an early age, most zero in on the most fragile child and give that hapless victim endless opportunities to practice self-defense. Unfortunately, most of these opportunities are unsuccessful, and the NLDer often returns from encounters with the neighborhood children broken both in body and in spirit.

Check out the games on the street, the kids riding bikes, the skateboarders scooting innocently by your front porch. Talk to them and try to meet their parents. Before you send your child outside to contend with the *dramatis personae* of childhood, make sure that he can read the script. It's true that all the world's a stage, but some children are a lot happier just sitting in the audience.

The most important room in the NLD-friendly home is the family room, the essence of the family's philosophy and spirit. In most families, this is the room that silently bears witness to the family's values and interests, hopes and dreams. Make sure that the family life you have chosen to represent includes the special assets and capabilities of your NLDer. Include an area in the family room that is not overwhelmingly stimulating, to facilitate the possibility of relaxation without sensory overload. Make sure to include a spot for some of your NLDer's special interests and pursuits, so that they won't find it necessary to leave the room in order to do the things they like best. Let your NLDer choose a family activity once in a while, even if it means the rest of you have to grit your teeth through yet another showing of *The Secret World of Sharks and Rays.*

Try to keep this room free of stress. If you have lessons to teach or conflict to resolve, schedule those moments in other parts of the house so that the family room remains a refuge for quiet, comfortable times. This does not mean that you should never reprimand your NLDer. On the contrary, it is critically important to set realistic expectations for every child in your care. NLDers, however, do not generalize from one incident to another. For this reason, it is your responsibility to help them learn from their mistakes not by punishing, but by gently pointing out where a better decision might have been made.

Although NLDers have difficulty connecting long-term consequences to actions, the ultimate connection is not an impossibility. It simply takes numerous repetitions to help them understand the possible results of their actions. Often, they are their own worst enemies because they cut off many conceivable positive outcomes by assuming that short-term consequences represent the full range of results. When poor social judgment is added to the mix, they are debilitated by the devastating combination of shortsightedness plus poor impulse control.

So if you want to have a true NLD-friendly home, you must learn to be a true friend to your NLDer by clarifying the non-negotiable rules for your family. If children in your household have chores to do, then make sure that your NLDer has chores as well. Don't let your child's disability be an excuse for poor manners, unseemly habits, inappropriate hygiene, or childish behavior. Make sure that your NLDer has a clear understanding of everything that is expected and a clear awareness of how to accomplish each expectation. Support every effort patiently and fill in the gaps unobtrusively as your NLDers work to achieve self-sufficiency.

Those of us who live in areas where winter snows often change our daily routines will understand the comparison of preparing your home for a child with NLD as you would prepare your vehicle for the upcoming winter. It would be patently irresponsible to make no advance preparations and just assume that the weather would be sunny and warm all winter. Those of us who want our cars to run smoothly through the winter make sure that before the threat of the first major storm, we winterize all the fluids, check the antifreeze, and make sure that the snow tires are in good condition. We would be foolish to start making plans only after it began to snow. When you live with a child with special needs, make sure that you are in no danger of careening into a ditch when it looks as though you're headed for a storm.

In addition to sturdy furniture, forgiving fabrics, and well-protected breakables, there are a few other ingredients which are critical for establishing an NLD-friendly home. Make sure to give your child the basic skills for independence and productivity. Add an enormous portion of patience. After you've stirred this into every facet of life, go back and add some more. You'll also need a hefty helping of hope to make sure that all your plans seem possible and realistic. Then go through every room looking for challenges and pitfalls. Every time you see something that might create a problem for your NLDer, sweeten the bitterness with a mammoth measure of unconditional love.

The classical musical *The Fantastiks* tells us: "Plant a radish, get a radish, not a brussels sprout…" Well, some of us might have been quite surprised by the varieties that popped up in our little family plots, but the classic rules of gardening still hold. Careful and consistent nurturing produces superstars. No one size, style, or shape is required for an NLD-friendly home. Like people with NLD, these homes come in all shapes, sizes, and colors. And just like people with NLD, they return untold rewards for the consistent investment of love and dedication.

Key points

1. Many children with NLD face daily discomfort and defeat in the outside world. Make sure that they find comfort and success at home. Involve the entire family in helping your NLDers know that they are understood and appreciated.

2. Go through your home from the perspective of your NLDer. Think about areas which could compromise your child's physical or emotional safety. Make sure that you know your child's preferences before you make any changes. When you have established what will make your children feel comfortable,

arrange your home to meet their needs without creating a fuss and without making announcements that call attention to their disabilities.

3. Check each room for possible pitfalls and challenges. Pay special attention to the bathroom, bedroom, kitchen, and family room. If it is impossible to remove all sensory challenges, create spaces where your NLDer can feel comfortable.

4. Make sure that your home is a place where expectations are clear, support is consistent and available, safety – both physical and emotional – is paramount, and unconditional love underlies every interaction.

Chapter Four

All in the Family

Perhaps the greatest social service that can be rendered by anybody to the country and to mankind is to bring up a family.

(George Bernard Shaw)

Have you tried to buy a mattress lately? Things have changed drastically from the days when our ancestors made a little pile of sand to cushion their heads at the dark end of the cave. Today we can choose from pillow-top, heat sensitive, latex, sleep number, air foam, and a range of other possibilities designed for our nocturnal pleasure and optimal bodily comfort. But learning specialist Rick Lavoie recommends only one bedtime option for families whose children have learning disabilities. Using a clear and powerful analogy, he suggests that such families sleep in a giant metaphorical waterbed. When the child with special needs flails about or rolls over, everyone in the family must readjust to compensate for the ensuing waves and ripples or risk spending the night on the hard cold floor (Lavoie 2003).

As the parents of children with NLD, most of us have learned by now that a child with a different style of living and learning cannot exist independently of family styles and rhythms. Neither can the family of such a child remain oblivious to their child's special style and rhythm. To expand Lavoie's metaphor, we should all be prepared for some unexpected waves and ripples, while ensuring simultaneously that no one gets abruptly ejected from the bed.

By the time a child is diagnosed with NLD, his or her parents have usually experienced a healthy period of oblivion or denial. If this is their first child, they may think it wonderful that their baby is so complacent and quiet, willing to sit patiently while curiously pointing at things he or she wants to name and know about. They may, in fact, find their progeny implausibly superior to the Glockenspiel baby next door, who prattles all over the house, pulling things off shelves and generally wreaking havoc with all unsecured knick-knacks, trinkets, and gadgets. And wasn't it a slap in the face to poor Mrs. G. when her baby just waved good-bye with a happy smile on the first day of preschool? Certainly you would expect a toddler who loved her mother to be at least as unsettled as Florinda, who wouldn't relinquish her blanket, her bottle, or her mother's leg for at least three quarters of an hour.

By the time Florinda starts school, members of her family might start to envy the Glockenspiels and their neurotypical child. Although there is nothing outwardly wrong with Florinda, and her pediatricians have assured everyone that nothing is developmentally abnormal, it seems that whatever Florinda does is just a little bit different or a little more difficult. Her doting parents may not have acknowledged their worries even to themselves, but Florinda seems to have a unique perspective which governs interactions with people, places, projects, and most of life's daily living requirements.

When Florinda is diagnosed with a nonverbal learning disability, at seven, or nine, or even twelve years old, her parents' fears for the future are sometimes accompanied by relief at having a label for what has always been referred to as: "Leave her alone. That's just Florinda's way of doing things." One college student in my practice disclosed the relief he experienced at being diagnosed with a learning disability after flunking out of a prestigious university. I had expected him to be angry or in denial, but he said that he had not been surprised at all to learn he had NLD. He was glad to have a name for all the learning problems he already knew he had. In fact, the diagnosis of NLD was actually better than he had expected, because at least this diagnosis included some assets along with the deficits.

But between the diagnosis and the ultimate acknowledgment that there is indeed a difference to accommodate, there is often a period of readjustment in the household while family members sift through feelings of guilt, blame, anger, denial, and acceptance. If these feelings sound similar to the five stages that Elizabeth Kübler-Ross attributes to family reactions preparing emotionally for the death of a loved one (denial, anger, bargaining, depression, and acceptance), that is no coincidence. A family must first mourn and bury their expectation of the perfect neurotypical child before fully accepting the wonderful child that they have – a wonderful child with nonverbal learning disabilities (Kübler-Ross 1997).

I noticed the similarity between the way families accept the news of a diagnosis of learning disability and the way families incorporate other bad news upon receiving my son's diagnosis in 1992. Initially I was relieved to discover that the irregular picture my son was presenting in school, in peer activities, and at home was due to a learning disability. Early in my career, I had spent sixteen years as a classroom teacher. I felt certain that there was no type of learning disability I couldn't help him overcome. Obviously, I knew nothing about NLD. As I began to read and familiarize myself with the syndrome, I became suffused with fear and dread. The charming little boy I had characterized as quirky and brilliant suddenly seemed like the character described in a nineteenth-century Gilbert and Sullivan operetta.

> In me there meet a combination of antithetical elements which are at eternal war with one another. Driven hither by objective influences – thither by subjective emotions – wafted one moment into blazing day by mocking hope – plunged the next into the Cimmerian darkness of tangible despair, I am but a living ganglion of irreconcilable antagonisms.

(Gilbert 2000)

I mourned for the future of my child. To make matters worse, when I recovered enough to enlist my husband in initiating the changes that would make our son feel loved, productive, and comfortable both at home and at school, I was met with a combination of disdain and disbelief.

Although he now understands our son as well as I do and probably interacts with him even more effectively, my husband found it difficult to accept the ramifications of his son's diagnosis. As I have stated, it is always difficult to accept any difference in a child which deviates from the idealized picture formed in a parent's mind. In our case, two older sons had already shown clear indications that they would be following nontraditional paths in life. Apparently my husband had been harboring certain conventional notions about father–son relationships that he hoped to realize with his youngest child. When issues arose which interfered with that plan, or which might render its execution more complex, he felt threatened.

My husband is a scientist, a physician's physician who is called in when other doctors don't know what course to pursue. He likes to develop a diagnosis through a series of empirical tests which produce incontrovertible results. Although parts of the NLD syndrome can be organically documented through neuropsychological testing, there are many "soft" neurological manifestations whose origins are hard to secure. For a long time, he accused me of making excuses for behaviors that I thought originated in the disability and that he believed were character flaws or simply signs of laziness.

Since I am an educator, my husband let me take the lead during the contentious sessions with school administrators, and gave himself permission to remain somewhat out of the loop. Finally, I made it clear to him that I was not involved in our child's case as a professional, but rather as a parent. I explained that, since it had been categorically impossible for me to create our child alone, I could no longer represent that child alone to the school.

Gradually, he began to see that the suggestions proposed by teachers and administrators were not only ludicrous, but actually harmful. After each encounter with the school system, my husband became more involved in our struggle. This process is not gender-specific. Often it is the father who is the primary advocate, while the mother stands back and learns to accept the whole picture with time and experience.

Acknowledging that your child has a learning disability means first accepting that part of the DNA you passed on was different or even defective. This may be harder for men who, like many NLDers, are prone to designating things as either all good or all bad. Although NLD can come from a number of genetic and serendipitous origins, many NLDers bear characteristics that one or both parents manifest. The difference is that neither parent has all of them together, and both have probably been able to compensate for their deficits without being overwhelmed. But it can be a rude awakening to see a mother's math phobia turn into a child's math disability or to see a father's need for "alone time" manifest as a total fear of interpersonal relationships that impairs a child's social life.

Ironically, keeping with the NLD tradition of assets and deficits, even the fact that some characteristics are passed down from one generation to another has a positive aspect. Many boys with NLD grow into men with nontraditional interests. They are rarely the type to sit around and watch the game with a "cold one." So it can be of benefit to both generations that, in families where such characteristics are inherited, boys who would rather watch a video on understanding opera, or kids who watch the latest version of Enterprise instead of the big game, may have fathers who prefer to do exactly the same thing.

But sometimes a guy who wants to throw a ball around in the back yard can sorely miss that type of companionship with his NLD child. So what do you do when you and your spouse come from totally different viewpoints? It helps to find a professional who can give you a third opinion about what is best for your child, as long as you both agree to accept it. Marriages or partnerships with a disabled child are at great risk. It is worth investing in discussing the reasons for the difference of opinion, even if you have to spend time and money on professional counseling. Most important, you must both agree to love your child and to present a united front even when there are backstage differences of opinion. Kids with NLD are very aware of environmental stress and fearful for their own emotional safety. If you believe that your spouse is resistant, perhaps he or she is simply undereducated.

Since children with NLD interpret things literally, they may actually fear for a parent's life when they hear one say to the other, "I could just kill you for being so stubborn about this!" If you are the one who has a better handle on this disorder, make some articles available to your spouse. Start with the short and direct ones before you move on to convoluted neuropsychology. Make a phone or personal appointment with an NLD coach or with a therapist who helps families work through the issues of families with children who have learning differences. You probably think you can work through things yourself. When you do, make sure to call the *Guinness Book of World Records*. They're still waiting for someone to fill this category.

Some spouses have astonishing endurance for denial. But if your child really has NLD, there will come a time when your spouse can no longer refuse to acknowledge the situation. When there's a wet dog in the room, sooner or later, everyone starts to recognize the smell. Even if the smell is initially subtle, most people become aware of it when the dog shakes cold, pungent, and muddy water all over them. You may feel resentful if you are the one called on to be patient at a time when you need patience and support from your loved ones. But in balanced relationships, couples should alternately assume the roles of giver and taker.

Make sure that you know how to give yourself healthy rewards for the extraordinary amounts of emotional and physical energy you are forced to generate every day. Your spouse may come to see the point sooner, later, or, in the worst and most unfair scenario, never. Sometimes you'll have to settle for having him or her simply love your child. Some spouses can't even get that far. If your minimum demands are not being met, I suggest you look in your local phone book under one of the following headings: Massage Therapy/In-Home, or Attorneys/Divorce.

If NLDers could be left to live happily in NLD Land, they would probably suffer minimal anxiety and enjoy maximum productivity. But instead, they live in a world where Grandma, Grandpa, and Aunt Raisinette want to know why Jerome always retreats to his room every time there is a family gathering. "And why does he mumble like that?" and "Why isn't he going to skateboarding camp with the rest of the cousins?" and "Can't you teach him to be a little more chatty instead of telling me all about school in two words?" and finally, "So when are we going to see a little girlfriend when we come to see you, huh?"

Siblings can be the cruelest. "You should have seen Hortense at softball practice, Mom. She was such a klutz that the coach asked if we came from the same genetic pool. She couldn't believe that we're fraternal twins, or whatever you call fraternal twins who are girls. Sisternal, I guess." In one of nature's cruelest twists, NLD often affects only one in a set of fraternal twins. Difficulties here arise from two reasons. Life can be complicated for the twins themselves, because the non-disabled twin may feel responsible for the other or, conversely, may want to destroy all birth records that attest to kinship. For parents, it can be heart-wrenching to see two children with such similar genetic backgrounds develop with such different assets and deficits.

So what do you tell aunts, uncles, sisters, brothers, and nosy neighbors? There is no hard-and-fast rule, of course, and some families choose never to disclose any information about a child's diagnosis of NLD outside of a therapeutic or educational setting. The decision to keep a secret, however, usually comes back to smack someone in the face. Although the smack might be intended to fall on an innocent bystander, you should consider this course of action most carefully, since your child may be its unwitting recipient.

Family members should be introduced to the syndrome of NLD and its manifestations in an age-appropriate manner, gradually, positively, and with clear, understandable information. There is no need to bombard Grandma and Grandpa with the neurobiological assets and their primary, secondary, and tertiary ramifications. It can sometimes be enough to say that Darwin has very acute responses to sound, touch, and light, so we try to surround him with the gentlest of behaviors and environments. Suggest that sneaking up behind him for a surprise bear hug is probably not a good idea. If you talk about a different aspect each time the grandparents visit, they'll gradually learn how to make little Dar happy before he barricades himself in his room at the first whiff of Grandma's cologne.

Remember to include a success each time you tell people of a difficulty. "Did I tell you that he is the only second grader who has never made an error on a spelling test?"

Encourage the siblings to understand the assets and deficits of NLD. When they are young, tell them that the NLDer is probably a great resource for spelling words, computer assistance, remembering what Mom or Dad promised about the family vacation next summer, and who owes exactly what sum of money or which collector's card to whom. Explain that they should notice if the NLDer needs help in the morning getting a coat, lunch, and bookbag together before the bus pulls away. Have some family talks about bullying and explain that bullies like to find people who are different because they are easy to bully.

Explain to all the siblings that kids with NLD might mumble a bit, some are a little clumsy, some have trouble keeping their shirts tucked in, and some like to talk about subjects that not everyone enjoys. For these reasons, NLDers often become the targets of bullies. Explain to all of your children the need to unite against bullies. Help them learn how to stand up to a bully safely. You can even arrange to have an outside curriculum against bullying visit your school.

Remember that siblings of a child who seems different or who is mocked in school may naturally wish that they could dissociate from the target of such negative attention. Rather than rush to help the sibling with NLD, they may run as far as possible in the opposite direction. Try to understand that this is a normal reaction. It affects the social position of neurotypical siblings as well, especially when children refuse to come over because they don't want to play with the NLDer. Some children feel conflicted and guilty because they see how difficult school can be for the sibling with NLD when they have relatively few problems socializing and studying.

At home, siblings may resent a brother or sister who seems to be receiving extra privileges. Because kids with NLD usually take longer than their neurotypical siblings to perform household tasks, they eventually receive fewer obligations at home and easier household chores. In the Sibling Wars, this can incite a major battle. If someone points out an inequity, it is a good idea to sit down and discuss who does what, how much energy each has to expend, who is good at what, and what will be best for the household in the long run.

When it was my NLDer's chore to set the table, we often ended up eating our dinner in various stages of lukewarm. Rushing down from his bedroom to set the table was not his forte. So we switched him to loading the dishwasher after dinner, which he accomplished in a reasonable time with supervision. The other siblings didn't have to sit and wait while this was done, so there were no recriminations if it took a little longer than expected. When the parent on dish duty saw that he needed some extra help, it was given quietly without having our three live-in inspectors from the Child Labor Fairness Committee scream, "You helped him! I saw! You never help me!"

It doesn't matter if you have fifteen children or your NLDer is an only child. You could probably get along without giving him or her the responsibility of a daily or weekly chore. But to exclude this child from what you expect of others is a concession to the disability that announces both to your child and to the world that you consider him or her a person of diminished capacity. Those of us who live with these perplexing and fascinating children know that sometimes it is easier to do the chore ourselves than to depend on their help. But it is definitely our responsibility as parents to make sure that they know how to handle basic household responsibilities.

If your child is a superstar at daily household maintenance, independent living can be a reality.

If you find that multistep directions cause problems, keep a file of chore cards with specific directions. For every task you expect your child to do, make a specific list of all steps from the beginning of the job to its completion. *Voilà!* Your NLDer will have no reason to protest, and you'll be surprised to see that even your neurotypical children will refer to the instructions.

Be more explicit than you think you need to be. Remember that when you are dealing with children who have NLD, you may think you shouldn't have to tell them, but you do. Here's an example of an instruction card for a household chore which you can adjust for age and level of capability:

Chore #3 – Setting the table for family dinner

1. If there are any books, papers, or magazines on the table, put them in a pile on the counter under the phone. Ask Mom or Dad where to put anything that is not a book, paper, or magazine. Clear everything else off the table.

2. Ask Mom or Dad how many people will be having dinner every time you set the table. Put a plate down for each person.

3. Go to the silverware drawer. For each person having dinner, get a fork, a knife, and a spoon. Take the silverware to the table. Put a fork at the left side of each plate. Then put a knife at the right side of the plate. Put the spoon to the right side of the knife. If it is a holiday or special dinner, ask Mom or Dad if there is any special silverware to add.

4. Get drinking glasses for each person having dinner. Put a glass at each place, above the knife.

5. Put this card back in the card file when you're done and tell Mom or Dad you're finished.

I must tell you that, in our house, when our NLDer sets the table, the fork goes on the right and the knife and spoon go on the left. An intelligent young adult, he has long been able to discriminate right from left. But his insistence on this method is based on logic. He argues that only one child in our family is left-handed. That child no longer lives at home. Therefore, it's counter-intuitive to put the fork on the left when you are going to use it with your right hand. This is one of the many NLD moments that each household chooses to handle in its own way. When we have dinner guests, I set the table in the conventional way to avoid having to explain to my guests the origin of our idiosyncratic pattern. But otherwise, my concession to convoluted logic costs me much less than years of psychotherapy and mood stabilizers. It is important, however, to choose concessions only in areas that cause no pain, have no far-reaching consequences, and do not further alienate the NLDer.

Of course, I have demanded that certain things be done simply because that is the accepted way. I argued for months when my son insisted on putting a period after every word in a sentence in first grade. "Mom," he insisted, "you do actually stop after every word and a period indicates a stop. You don't say a whole sentence in a single breath." Finally we compromised by allowing him to use his unique punctuation system for personal papers (journal, letters, notes, etc.) as long as he acquiesced to the universally accepted system for school assignments.

The silverware argument is in the same category. These are NLD moments. You have to pick your arguments. If ever something of great importance hinges on our silverware placement, I will make sure that someone more conventional has the obligation of setting the table. For the time being, I will refuse to buck the great wall of logic over the location of a fork. Now that he is away at college, I sometimes look at the table and wonder why things seem a bit out of place. Then I remember. The table is set correctly.

When you "catch" your NLDer doing something right, make sure you're there with appropriate praise. Don't lavish disproportionate commendation on a teenager for completing a task that a six-year-old can do. You will do more harm by infantilizing your NLDers than by not complimenting them at all. But make sure they always know that you appreciate how much work they invest in activities that might seem effortless to others. Know where to praise and know where to correct. If something is not done right, start by discussing a part of the process that has been done well. Then make a concrete suggestion for improving performance the next time.

There are certain responsibilities for parents and families of NLDers that are absolutely non-negotiable. If you want your child to live and interact safely outside of your home, you must make sure that he or she can manage the basic requirements of daily living. You must make sure that he or she knows how to eat appropriately, knows how to speak and be understood, knows how to handle basic monetary transactions, knows how to advocate for and request whatever is needed, knows how to say "thank you," and knows how to say "no."

You should train your child from an early age to discriminate between people who just seem nice and people who truly are nice. Watch television shows or movies with your child and engage in dialogue about social situations you see. "What kind of neighbor do you think Mr. Wilson is? Do you think he is being nice to Dennis or should Dennis stay away from him?" "Do you think Huey, Dewey, and Louie should apologize to Uncle Donald? They really got in a lot of trouble today!"

Explain to relatives, friends, and siblings that your child interprets things in a very literal manner. Although we often laugh at the way children with NLD misinterpret things, it is often a sad demonstration of the effect their disability has on language pragmatics. Recently I learned of a child who asked his mother to put bottled water in his school lunches. Dutifully, she went out and bought several cases of pure spring water and stored them where she could comfortably pack a bottle each day. As the beginning of the school year approached, her son became increasingly apprehensive about his drinks for school. Aware of his tendency to perseverate, she gently reassured him that everything was taken care of. Finally, he was no longer able to contain his anxiety. "But Mom," he worried, "those bottles all say 'spring water.' What am I going to drink in the fall?"

Teach your child to laugh. While most families ultimately develop a communal sense of humor, it is hard to know whether this is related to events that all have experienced, specific neurological wiring, cultural conditioning, or genetics. Although it may seem difficult to conceive of a genetic sense of humor, adoption specialists report that this is one problem which tends to make children feel alienated from their adoptive families.

Even children adopted as infants just can't understand some of the things that seem to drive their adoptive parents and siblings into paroxysms of laughter. Children with NLD often find themselves in a similar situation. Because their brains are uniquely "wired," they are liable to interpret humor differently from other members of the family.

In fact, many studies suggest that NLDers have no sense of humor, but I find that the opposite is true. Every child or adult with NLD whom I have come to know possesses a dry incisive wit and an idiosyncratic distinction about what is funny. I have watched my own son bellow his monotonic guffaw at television shows or print cartoons that I find no funnier than an itch in a place I can't reach. They may miss certain comedic references that are inferred, rather than explicit, and there may be some characters with problems so close to their own that they don't seem funny. But humor is a healthy outlet for NLDers. You should encourage your children to find the things that make them laugh, as long as the laughter is not derived at the expense of other human beings.

For children with NLD, the world can be a confusing and often frightening place. They work incredibly hard to keep up with the behaviors and responsibilities that are imposed upon them when they are away from home. Some literally count the minutes until they can step off that school bus and get back to safe and familiar territory. Yet many behave like angels at school and turn into holy terrors at home.

Ironically, this happens because home is the safest place for them to decompensate. Give them space and time for re-entry. Don't bombard your child with questions and responsibilities for at least an hour after school. For some of us, the hardest component of being part of an NLD family is knowing when to offer nothing but silence, a snack, and a smile.

Tolstoy wrote that all happy families resemble each other (Tolstoy 1997). Obviously he had never encountered anyone with NLD. Just as each NLDer is unique, so is each NLDer's family. Happy NLD families might not resemble each other, but they can all learn to develop a fully functional and rewarding lifestyle that provides safety and consistency for the child with NLD, fairness and understanding for every child, and patience, love, and respect for all.

Key points

1. Share the parenting. Share the pleasure and the pain. Explain the assets and deficits of NLD to siblings, family, and friends.

2. Remember that all children deserve to be given the basic non-negotiable skills for integrating successfully into neurotypical society. You must make sure that they know how to eat appropriately, know how to speak and be understood, know how to handle basic monetary transactions, know how to advocate for and request whatever is needed, know how to say "thank you," and know how to say "no."

3. Teach your NLDer to laugh and enjoy life. Do everything you can to prevent the dour and pessimistic mindset that is the natural default of many children with NLD.

4. All happy families are not the same, but they share similar principles. They all consider the needs and support the interests of every family member. They make time to listen to everyone's concerns and try to accommodate all appropriate wishes. They operate on a foundation of love and respect.

Chapter Five

Making Sense of the Senses

Many of you may not have read the fundamental tractates on the origins of NLD. There are those that suggest it results from trauma to the right hemisphere, from faulty connectivity between the two hemispheres, from damage to the myelin, from insufficiency of the corpus callosum, and from many other neurobiological hypotheses already proposed and yet to come. One day, when neurobiological technology makes it simple for scientists to watch the human brain in operation as people with NLD perform functions of daily living, we may know how the NLD brain really works. But until that time, I prefer to attribute the mystery to the story documented below. There's great dispute concerning the provenance and authenticity of this elemental saga, so rather than side with one camp or another, I will give an objective summary. Those of you who live with and love people with NLD can draw your own conclusions.

It is told that after the Higher Power finished creating the neurotypical prototype of man and woman, there was time in the Creation Cycle to add change and challenge to the human condition. So the Higher Power unleashed all sorts of imaginative freedom and developed models for human beings who would populate the Earth as the generations evolved. This resourceful vitality engendered people of diverse ethnicities, opinions, talents, and capabilities, so that as the world grew, every need on earth could be addressed by its inhabitants. So that everything could find wholeness and completion, each creation had its counterpart. For the darkness there was light; for ugliness, beauty; for warmth, cold; and for the left, the right. For the arguer, the Higher Power created the conciliator; for the anxious, the soother; and for the noisy, the silent. For all types of learners, too, the Higher Power created counterparts, so that all people could have a chance to enjoy the world in which they lived. For those who had difficulty learning to read, there were those who loved to teach them; for those who had difficulty smiling, there were those who loved to make them laugh. The Higher Power was busy, busy, busy, and hardly noticed that the special wrinkle in time sheltered for the Creation Cycle was coming to a close. All of the Higher Power's assistants (known as the Highered Help) began urging wildly that all creations be completed before the Creation Cycle ended, lest they be left unfinished.

At just about this time, in the twilight of the Creation Cycle, the Higher Power was busy creating a fascinating brain design called the NLD proto-type. People with this type of learning power would have incredible assets: rote memory skills, phenomenal vocabularies, and expressive language skills. They would be blessed with a true sense of integrity and justice, and the ability to discern and isolate important facts. The Higher Power was just filling in the details as dusk began to fall on the last day of the Creation Cycle.

"Quickly!" urged the Highered Help. "What about the sensory details? What about meltdowns, shutdowns? Do you want them to have control over these types of things?"

The Higher Power needed to ponder. His audible muttering began to resonate through the Universe. "Ahhhhhhhhhhhhh…"

But suddenly blinding flashes of lightning and clamorous bolts of thunder signaled the end of the Creation Cycle. The Highered Help could hardly hear what was being said. In fact, they thought the Higher Power was saying, "Nahhhhhhhhhhhhh."

Suddenly the curtain lending light to the Creation closed with a bang. Before the NLDers had been given all of their assets, their powers were inadvertently circumscribed. And to make matters even more challenging, the Highered Help had mistakenly and irrevocably given NLDers disorders of sensory integration, including a prodigious propensity for shutdowns and meltdowns.

So it is today that people with NLD have not only assets, but deficits as well. But the Higher Power, to make up for the inability to create them according to the fullest conception, has always granted people with NLD a special celestial care and protection. And that, some say, is the greatest asset of all.

There are three main questions for the families of NLDers to address concerning disorders of sensory integration. The first, not surprisingly, is "What *is* sensory integration?" It really helps to know what it is that can wreak such havoc when it is disordered and to understand the norm we hope to restore. The second question is "How is sensory integration related to NLD?" If we don't understand the fundamental connection between disorders of sensory integration and nonverbal learning disorders, we might as well be talking about poison ivy, because, after all, kids with NLD can get poison ivy, too. And third, "After I learn about disorders of sensory integration and their relation to NLD, how can I minimize their effect on my child?"

What is sensory integration?

We all know that human beings experience the world through senses of vision, hearing, taste, touch, and smell. We also use the vestibular sense, which makes us aware of gravity and movement, and the proprioceptive sense, which relays information about our muscles, joints, and ligaments. When the intact sensory system receives messages from internal and external environments, it processes them smoothly and immediately, and then directs the information to the appropriate parts of the brain. The brain synthesizes or integrates the information and enables the individual to respond to the stimuli in the appropriate manner.

In some people, however, there is a disturbance in the capacity to automatically integrate and respond appropriately. This individual is said to have a disorder of sensory integration (DSI), or sensory integration dysfunction. This disorder can have a serious and negative impact on the tasks of daily living by affecting a person's capacity to learn and to function in society. Like NLD, DSI is a complex neurological disorder. Some people with DSI are *hyposensitive*, meaning that they are under-responsive to sensation. Since they naturally seek out sensory experiences that are more intense or of longer duration, they often engage in hyperactivity as they seek more and more sensory input from movement. They may have a lack of awareness to touch or pain, or the inability to discern when they are touching others too often or too hard. Some enjoy sounds that are too loud, such as high volume on the TV, stereo, or radio. Still others engage in unsafe behaviors, such as climbing too high, in order to achieve the sensation that people with neurotypical sensory systems can derive from less risky behaviors.

Other people with DSI are *hypersensitive*. They are overly reactive to stimuli, with nervous systems that feel sensation too easily or too intensely. Since they are so overly responsive to sensation, they may experience "fight or flight" responses, a condition called "sensory defensiveness." As children, and probably as adults, these people are usually afraid of touch and respond to being touched with aggression or withdrawal. They are afraid of movement and heights, and are usually extremely cautious about trying new things or taking risks. Some, in fact, are completely unwilling to do so. Generally, people who are hypersensitive are overwhelmed in loud or busy environments such as sports events or malls. They are very picky eaters and are usually overly sensitive to smells, especially smells related to food.

The third category of DSI is related to dyspraxia, which affects motor skills and activities. These children are generally clumsy, and have poor fine motor skills. Many have graphomotor difficulties, which is often noticed in school as they begin to learn to write. They show early difficulties in games such as "Simon Says," where motor skills and instructions must work together. They are challenged by activities requiring balance, motor sequence, and bilateral coordination (The KID Foundation 2003).

How is sensory integration related to NLD?

Although not all people with DSI have NLD, many children who are ultimately diagnosed with NLD begin their journey toward diagnosis with the early presentation of symptoms in the category of sensory dysfunction. It is also important to remember that, although most people with NLD have some element of sensory dysfunction, the range and degree can vary greatly. When the brain does not process sensory information efficiently, due to a disturbance in the right hemisphere such as that believed to cause NLD or any other neurological processing disorder, the feedback is inconsistent and sometimes incorrect. This inappropriate feedback causes any combination of the behaviors above which are included in the category of DSI, which is a major player in the deficit profile of the syndrome of NLD.

After I learn about disorders of sensory integration and their relation to NLD, how can I minimize their effect on my child?

In school and at home, it is best to prepare an environment for the NLDer which has minimal sensory stimuli. Visual clutter can cause sensory distraction, as can the auditory hum and visual flicker of fluorescent lighting. Even though you can't imagine being disturbed by some of the things your children mention, take their word as gospel. Make sure that everything they consider a distraction is removed from their environments to minimize meltdowns. It will be much easier to control a sensory-safe environment at home, where you can regulate the decibel and brightness level.

If a school is unwilling or unable to regulate the tone of public announcements, fire drill alarms, band practice, choir, etc., find a comfortable pair of ear plugs for your child to use. This, too, will be a period of sensory trial. There are all kinds with which to experiment – plastic, wax, silicone, rubber, and probably other types of synthetic that haven't even been named yet. One child I know wears earphones in school. They're not plugged to anything but his brain, but they manage to muffle distracting environmental sounds and he believes that he looks cool wearing them.

Neurotypical children and adults have many ways to deal with sensory overload. When the left hemisphere begins to feel stressed, we use soothing, coping, and rationalizing mechanisms generated in the right hemisphere to help deflect antisocial behavior. Some children who need sensory soothing, even when they are very young, can find quirky and creative ways to get the feedback that their central nervous system desires.

A colleague of mine was forced to take her four-year-old son along when trying to find an agent to represent her artwork. He entertained himself quietly through most of the interview when he was suddenly seized by the need to remove all of his clothes. Luckily, in the artistic environment of agents and artists, no one considered this behavior much outside the norm. Mom and the prospective agent continued talking as the resourceful little boy rifled through her bag for something that would make him feel just right. Casting off all sorts of toys, books, and educational projects, he discovered a pair of panty hose that his mother had removed right before the interview when she noticed a run.

With great concentration, he managed awkwardly to jam his little limbs into the appropriate openings and ultimately pulled the waistband up over his head. Without realizing that he had invented the home-grown version of an occupational therapist's body sock, our naked adventurer immediately settled into a routine of sensory decompensation which allowed his mother to finish the interview. The agent ultimately agreed to represent her, and the little boy grew into a strapping six-footer. As a college wrestler and football player, he still gets to enjoy the feeling of tight pants, but manages to look a bit more gender-appropriate.

Although some people who experience disorders of sensory integration are lucky enough to find solutions for the feelings of discomfort they experience, most children and adults with NLD have only two methods for dealing with sensory overload: they melt down or they shut down. Sensory overload occurs when the brain is confronted with more information than it can handle at one time. Although a meltdown may seem like a destructive act, it is really an act of self-defense. The brain is saying in its clearest and most dynamic form, "I cannot tolerate this. Stop or I will self-destruct."

Once the neurons have been given the signal to melt down, the process is similar to the launch of a ballistic missile. You must wait until it is over and hope that the missile has not landed in the midst of a densely populated area. Many parents swear that the meltdown and its characteristic tantrum come out of nowhere, but this is far from true. By careful observation of the patterns and triggers of meltdown behaviors, parents, educators, and caregivers can learn to recognize the preliminary "brownout" and intervene before the full meltdown process has begun.

The process of shutdown is also a defense to sensory bombardment, but it is a cumulative process which takes time to become apparent. In order to protect himself or herself from environmental stimuli which are uncomfortable, the NLDer gradually closes areas of response and function, until he or she is no longer participating in or responding to any of the relevant functions of age-appropriate life.

Did you ever dream how it might be to take a family vacation with neurotypical children? I don't think it's total fantasy because I see representatives of this rare species every time I venture forth into the unprotected world of people who travel without a fifteen-pound kit of quasi-medical devices and intervention ploys. Join me as I fantasize. A family sits around the table – Mom, Dad, and three little lovelies. Dinner has just been consumed, but no one is covered with lingering *eau de pea.* Everyone has enjoyed the same meal, said "thank you," and helped with the dishes.

Since the kids had completed their homework in the afternoon, the family can sit together to discuss their annual vacation. After a civil and caring discussion of likes and dislikes, all agree on a fun-filled vacation spot which has loads of activities for the little darlings and even some romantic places for Mom and Dad to share an uninterrupted moment. (Those who cannot understand the concept "uninterrupted moment," just continue reading. You're in the right book.)

Fast forward to departure day. The children traipse happily down the stairs with their little carry-ons. No one had to call ahead to ask about fluorescent lighting, the temperature of the indoor and outdoor pools, or the description of the bedding on the Mohs hardness scale. No one had to carefully screen the children's travel garb for textures that might be scratchy, itchy, waxy, slimy, or otherwise uncomfortable. All they had to do was pack.

This fantasy was brought to you by NKTV, the neurotypical kids network. The station doesn't come in very well, and not very often, either. In fact, more families travel like a pack of NLDers than not, even though they're just providing for possibilities. The families of NLDers, however, know well in advance that they will need every precaution and post-traumatic palliative they've packed.

It is too simplistic to consider hyper- or hyposensitivity to sounds, light, and texture the entire picture of sensory dysfunction. DSI can extend to eating problems when children become fearful of new smells, tastes, and textures (see Chapter 7). Serious problems with sleep can develop from the need to have consistent linens, pillows, and bedmates (of the latter, most remain stuffed until a certain age).

Although all children display an unusually brief tolerance for standing in line, you will soon learn that there is no word ephemeral enough to describe the NLDer's capacity for waiting. By the time you pronounce the word "evanescent," the window of opportunity has slammed shut. Since NLDers have trouble understanding the consequences of an action, it is hard for them to understand the reasons for waiting in line. Also, they are unable to see the logic behind such a purposeless pastime. Frankly, if things functioned as they should, there would be no need for such time-wasting activity. Perhaps we need more NLDers in administrative and organizational positions. Until that time, however, remember to bring things which will keep your children happily occupied if you suspect that you might have to wait somewhere. Tell them in advance that this might happen, so they won't be confronted with an unsuspected change of plans.

When I was young and critical, I often found myself a few rows behind a family who brought a "bag of goodies" for their children when they came to services to observe the Jewish high holidays. This is the one time of year when most of us have the poor judgment to dress our offspring in ridiculously uncomfortable clothing and expect them to sit like angels through hours of what is surely meaningless intonation to children. Pinching new shoes, scratchy collars, and all sorts of sartorial suffering add to their distress. Nevertheless, I had the temerity to consider the family that brought a bag of books, quiet games, bottled water, sensory toys, and some non-crunchy munchies for their kids sacrilegious.

Over the years, I have come to realize that what they did was not blasphemous but blessed! I am so grateful that Judaism gives us Days of Penitence each year to ask forgiveness for the sins we have committed in years before. I now actually recommend that young families follow this procedure, for whatever formal occasion demands a modicum of quiet not usually required of our kids. "Save it for special occasions," I suggest. "Put something in there to make your son forget he is being 'choked' by a tie or to make your daughter forget that her legs are 'imprisoned' in tights." Some call this a "Proprioceptive Prop" or "Sensory Toolkit." I'm not so fussy. I just call it "Oh Holy Bag."

The best way to help your child cope with DSI is to read everything you can about this disorder and try to anticipate what will make your child uncomfortable, and, conversely, what will make your child feel less anxious. If you can identify difficult situations in advance, you can avoid or modify them. Understanding your child's reactions will also help you from reacting adversely to things that he or she does which are unavoidable neurological responses and not volitional annoying behaviors.

Occupational therapists are incredible at helping families and children with DSI learn to make peace with the obstacle course of daily living. However, parents who know their children are also incredibly inventive in devising interventions that make life tolerable for both parent and child. One mother described each trip with her son to the grocery store as a high-speed episode of *Supermarket Sweep* as she ran down the aisles trying to get representatives of the five basic food groups into her cart before her son erupted into the inevitable high-decibel full-fledged meltdown. Then she realized that giving him a cookie before Aisle Number One would give her enough time to pick up a few things in relative calm. Even better, she discovered that giving him a blow pop would give her almost twenty minutes of uninterrupted shopping time. Wisely, she used something to calm his senses of smell, touch, and taste to deflect attention from the distracting visual and auditory stimulation of the grocery store.

When children are older, you can ask if they would like to help you with your task in a store or if they would prefer to sit by the entrance and listen to a book on tape or music on headphones or (if they are old enough) remain in the car. Explaining that you can accomplish things in half the time if you divide the list often encourages older children with NLD and young teens to offer their assistance. When your NLDer has done something helpful, make sure to offer age-appropriate praise. Reinforcing positive activities encourages them to try it again and builds confidence in their ability to be contributing members of the family.

The most important thing you can do if you suspect that your child has a disorder of sensory integration is to have a professional and thorough evaluation done by an occupational therapist who has experience with nonverbal learning disorders. Be an informed consumer before you select the professional who will work with your child. Don't be embarrassed to ask if the occupational therapist has had experience in working with children who have this disorder. Since it is a low-incidence disorder, not everyone is aware of its ramifications. The wrong intervention can be worse than the disorder!

Read Carol Kranowitz's (1998) seminal work, *The Out-of-Sync Child*. You may recognize your own child in there, and that recognition can only lead you to new awareness and help. Start thinking about your own sensory issues. Learn to be aware of how your body responds to sights, sounds, tastes, touch and smell, the vestibular sense, and proprioception. The more you know about your own responses, the more you will be able to understand your child.

Once a young man with NLD called home from boarding school. There was to be a formal assembly at school that week, and as his mother had come to expect, he had lost one of the components of the required dress code. The highly evolved mother of a teen NLDer, she responded in a calm, nurturing manner. "HOW MANY TIMES…?" I mean, "What is it that you need this time, dear? Have you misplaced your school tie, or the blazer? Is it your dress shoes?" No, this time it was the gray pants. The mother replaced the receiver and emitted a lengthy primordial sigh; not one of relief, I might add. Then she allowed herself a moment of blissful imagination where, as the mother of a neurotypical child, she could have called a catalogue and had them ship a pair of gray pants in her son's size directly to the school in time for the assembly. As soon as the reverie ended, she got to work.

The mother went to six stores. At each, she had one mission and one mission only – find a pair of gray dress slacks in size 38/34. One pair had cuffs. One pair was cotton, another synthetic. One pair was pleated, another had a flat front. One had some elastic in the waist. One had a button closure, one closed with a snap. Each had a bit of variation in the length of the rise, the width of the waistband, the lining or lack of it, the fabric, the size of the belt loops, and the type of closure above the fly. She fed the cats, called her husband at work, and set out to drive across the state, her bounty beside her. Hours later, she arrived at her son's school. Of course, he had expected her. With less patience than he should have displayed (since this was, after all, his dilemma), he tried on pair after pair, like a gargantuan Goldilocks.

"These itch. These pinch in the butt. This fabric hangs funny around the knees. This pair is too hard to button. I don't like the pleats." The commentary went on and on. Finally, Mom heard music to her ears. "These are okay."

Back into the bags went the other pairs of pants. Back across the state drove Mom. Back to the stores went the itchy, the baggy, the pleated, and the pinchers, to wait for other gentlemen six foot four with less pronounced sensory challenges. Back home went Mom and straight into bed. Thus ends the tale of the NLDer and the gray pants. No FedEx from the Gap for this guy. But Mom loves her NLDer and understands that he wasn't being difficult. He simply could not wear any of the others because his brain wouldn't allow his body to accept them.

P.S. Mom had gone to sleep without listening to her answering machine. In the morning, she heard this message: "Uh, thanks, Mom. For the pants, I mean. Bye."

Key points

1.   In order to understand your NLDer's sensory issues, you must be able to answer:

    ○ What is sensory integration?

    ○ How is sensory integration related to NLD?

    ○ How can I minimize the way that sensory integration disorder affects my child?

2.   There are three categories of sensory integration disorder:

    ○ *hypersensitivity* – the condition of being over-reactive to sensory input

    ○ *hyposensitivity* – the condition of being under-reactive to sensory input

    ○ *dyspraxia* – the condition of sensorimotor clumsiness.

3.   Sensory overload occurs when the brain is confronted with more information than it can handle at one time. Although a meltdown or shutdown may seem like a destructive act, it is really an act of self-defense. The brain is saying in its clearest and most dynamic form, "I cannot tolerate this. Stop or I will self-destruct."

4.   Children who complain of sensory problems are not being manipulative or cantankerous. They are experiencing true discomfort of neurological origin. There is no way to bribe them or coerce them out of their discomfort.

Chapter Six

School

School. Public, private, residential, parochial, charter, magnet, even homeschool. All the events leading up to it and winding down from it instill terror in the hearts of those who care for children with NLD. And for the children themselves, school can be even more terrifying. In fact, it is often the most difficult and frustrating sustained experience they face in their lives. For some children with NLD, it is the fundamental point of the anxiety around which they construct the disabling characteristics of this syndrome. These children focus almost all of their thoughts and actions, both in and out of the classroom, on the cognitive, social, and emotional relationships engendered by the seemingly ordinary business of acquiring an education.

Over the past twenty years, I have watched the yellow school bus ferry four children to untold terror and delight. For the first few days of each new school year, I would accompany my three older children to the bus stop, waiting as they bounded aboard amid a cacophony of greetings. Displaying various levels of self-confidence, depending on their ages, stages, or even fashion rages, they negotiated the aisles and offers of expectant seat-mates until they were fully invested in age-appropriate chit-chat or chicanery. Slyly, they would glance out the window, begging me silently, with eloquent eyes, not to wave or, even worse, blow kisses or utter anything motherly that

someone else might hear. Slightly saddened, but immensely relieved by their normal separation and engagement behaviors, I would return home or leave for work. Until the final school bell, I functioned in a grown-up world, disturbed only by the occasional early dismissal for an imminent blizzard or a day at home for some pediatric pampering.

When the older boys were in high school and my daughter was in middle school, my youngest child started kindergarten. It took me a few weeks to master the omnipresent desire to throw 20 or 30 tranquilizers into my morning coffee when I learned that the older boys would be riding to school with their friends who were already driving. Dad took the morning carpool to middle school, so my primary responsibility was helping the youngest get ready for kindergarten.

The older three, now into elaborate adolescent rituals involving hair gel and other more puzzling products, had developed an elaborate schedule for showers in their bathroom. I never had to worry that any of them would oversleep, because that might mean missing a millisecond of mirror time. Dad hates to get up in the morning, but is blessed with an extremely hyperfunctional sense of responsibility, so he was crisply dressed and ready even before the kids started fighting over water like thirsty desert dwellers at an oasis. I am an early riser who often paces nervously at the front door for the paper boy to deliver the morning edition at 5:30 a.m.

Through all of this, from cocoa to coffee, from health foods to frosted flakes, from the vegetarian of the moment to the steak and eggs brigade, the youngest slept undisturbed. No amount of noise, no alarm clock, no activity would wake him. Often I asked the older boys to hold him under his arms while I pulled off his pajamas and popped him into the tub for a quick sponge bath. He usually woke up, duly enraged, when the washcloth landed on his face. I then dried his semi-conscious six-year-old body and helped him pull his clothes on. If I left the room for a moment and said, "I'll meet you in the kitchen," he would crawl right back into bed. This exercise was repeated as many times as possible until I could drag him bodily down to the kitchen for some breakfast.

After I felt that he had ingested the minimum required dietary allotment which would absolve me from child abuse on the count of starvation, I began to negotiate the "getting ready for school" phase. Even when I had summoned the foresight to lay things out the night before, this child's belongings had a way of disappearing. When there was snow up to his kneecaps, his boots were always in school. Although I habitually bought four pair of the same mittens, I could never find more than one at any given time. I usually had plenty of things on hand to keep his head warm, but I was afraid that neighbors would call the police from the screaming that ensued when I tried to induce him to wear one of the itchy, scratchy, tight, blinding, pressing, headache-inducing Antarctic-tested torture chambers commonly known as hats. When it was 80 degrees out, though, my weather-unconscious child would often insist on wearing his soft, worn-in-by-two-brothers, wide-wale green corduroy pants or a nice fleece jacket. He didn't seem to be aware of his own internal temperature modulator, even when his lips were blue or his face looked like the prize tomato at the country fair.

Naïvely, I used to employ logic. "Well, it's a bit too warm outside for that today," or "We'd be better off saving that for a really cold day." When the pediatrician promised that not too many children died of heatstroke or frostbite in temperate climates from being slightly under- or over-dressed, I simply gave up. Some days, he looked like Nanook of the North on a trip to the Sahara desert, but ultimately we did move in the direction of the school.

At this pace, before I understood that people with NLD are absolutely incapable of hurrying or being hurried, we usually rounded the corner just in time to see the back row children waving from the kindergarten bus. "Caution, Carrying School Children," the inscription mocked as it moved farther and farther down the street. "No problem," I kept telling myself, as we strolled back to the car. "We'll just drive over and then I can drop him off and make sure that he gets to exactly the right door."

Secretly, I was relieved every time we missed the bus. I knew that this child didn't have the skills to board the bus, observe the scene, calculate the odds, make a decision, navigate the aisles, take charge of his equipment, and do everything in reverse when he arrived at the school. By the second month of kindergarten, we never even started out for the corner. Modifications for NLD begin early. In my son's case, they started four years before the official diagnosis.

Although the syndrome of NLD can have ramifications that extend far beyond the classroom, NLD is considered a learning disability because people with the diagnosis find new learning difficult, they over-rely on previously learned information, have deficiencies in learning due to lack of adaptability, and are not capable of intermodal integration when processing information. In fact, when first identifying the syndrome from a study of learning disability subtypes, Byron Rourke ascertained that the subjects employed in his original investigations met fairly standard criteria for inclusion in research of students classified as learning disabled. The students with the subtype of disability he ultimately classified as NLD were all markedly deficient in at least one school subject area. They tested within the roughly normal range on standardized IQ tests, were free of primary emotional disturbance, had adequate vision and hearing, did not suffer from educational deficits due to socioeconomic deprivation, had not experienced any unusual childhood illnesses, and had attended school regularly since they were five-and-a-half or six years old (Rourke 1995).

But for children with NLD, accommodation and remediation go far beyond the classroom. In order to help the child with NLD adjust to the world, every point of contact with that world must be explained within its idiosyncratic context. And it is not enough to make those explanations on Monday and assume that they will hold for Tuesday or Wednesday. The explanations must be consistent and constant – daily, weekly, monthly, and year after year – until, by a combination of repetition, maturity, time, and sheer willpower, they become a default reality which can be activated when the autonomic system doesn't make sense in the neurotypical world.

Because schools, educators, and special education professionals are more aware of language-based learning differences than they are of NLD, it is the job of every parent whose child carries this complex diagnosis to become a full-time advocate. The parents of children with NLD must proactively monitor the learning environment which delivers not only academic information, but also attitude, awareness, and ambience to the child with NLD. If you are the type of parent who has previously approached school administrators and faculty members like a shrinking violet, now is the time to reconfigure your roots. Have you ever heard of the lyrical fairy apron or the colorful rainbow plant? Model your actions after those species instead. They are carniverous plants. If you don't guard your children's rights with as strong a defense as these plants employ, your children will be the ones eaten alive by the school system.

There are many ways to obtain support services for your child, and since they are specific to different states and countries, the specifics will not be described here. However, the place to start is at the point of critical contact, in your child's classroom. Once you know what accommodations make your child comfortable and which conditions elicit optimal attention and productivity, talk to the teacher and see how these conditions can be arranged in class. Bring a short brochure or article explaining the basic assets and deficits of NLD. Stress the fact that your child loves to learn, is never oppositional by choice, and can be a contributing member to the classroom community as long as learning needs are met.

Some teachers will be more than willing to cooperate. There are truly wonderful people out there who are devoted to the profession of making the world an accessible and fascinating place for children to explore. But others will inform you that it is impossible to deviate from the norm for one child who needs quirky conditions for learning. Keep smiling. The penalties for teachercide are universally harsh, though I have met many who have made me seriously consider serving the time. Whatever the teacher's decision, most important is that you need to be there for your child, and it is even more difficult to raise a child with special needs from a prison cell.

If a teacher is unwilling or unable to make the modifications you need, go to the next level of authority. Keep going up the ladder patiently and politely until you reach the point of no return. At that juncture, you will have to decide if you should consider an external placement for your child, or if you will bring suit against the school system for not providing the accommodations which will help your child learn. In the United States, every child is guaranteed a free and appropriate public education in the least restrictive environment. However, the law is useless if there is no school near you in which this right can be enforced. Remember, too, that the time you spend defending your rights may be time your child loses in an inappropriate educational environment.

Assuming that you have somehow found a school or alternative learning set-up which works for your child, it is important to remember that children with NLD are not the ones you drop off at the door in kindergarten and think about again just as they are trying on caps and gowns for high-school graduation. Here are some guidelines to implement along the way in an attempt to minimize some of the expected problems of NLDers throughout their elementary and secondary school years.

From kindergarten through college, these children have a primary problem with organization. Some can ultimately learn the basic skills of keeping a datebook. Others can even be taught to devise a system for filing homework in such a way that the assignments actually surface close to the time they are due at school. But the moment you remove the supports which are bolstering these systems, whether they are electronic, human, or extra-terrestrial, the entire system is likely to implode.

For children with NLD, the organizational parts of the brain are like a student who has been physically injured in an accident and must learn to use a wheelchair for mobility. That student is highly motivated to gain access and movement, so is happy to work hard learning to use the chair, studying accessibility charts and memorizing accessible entrances and the location of ramps and elevators. But what would happen if, as soon as people saw that this student has gained accessibility, they said, "Well, congratulations, you know all about accessibility now, so we're taking away the ramps!" The injured student would no longer be able to get in. So, too, for the student with NLD. Although it may look as though he or she has mastered the use of organizational systems, he or she can never access them without the ramps. NLD is a lifelong neurological disability. The need for support is permanent and non-negotiable.

In kindergarten, whichever parent is on morning duty has to know where the essentials are – from muffins to mittens. As the student moves from grade to grade, the duties increase. Don't berate your children for not being able to do something which they are congenitally unable to do. Their frontal lobes are in wheelchairs. However, if you help them get up the ramp, they will be fine once they are inside the building.

If you are looking at after-school programs for children in preschool and elementary grades, make sure that these programs are operated by people who are both sophisticated and caring enough to facilitate your child's unique needs. Children with NLD spend so much time and energy understanding the world each day that they really need time to decompensate after school. They need to rest in an environment which does not overstimulate any of their sensory modalities. Parents should evaluate the temperaments and interests of other children in the program. As convenient as it might be to keep Waldo in school for several more hours, if he is with a group of bullies who traumatize him for watching *Teletubbies* while they are devotees of *The Man Show*, the time you save will cost you geometric multiples more in the long run.

Although elementary school will present sensory and cognitive issues unique to each child's NLD "package," the universal problem with which most struggle is homework. This is an issue which is best worked out on an individual basis once you have gained the sympathy of the classroom teacher or special education director. The following points, however, are important to consider when you are helping the school develop your child's homework policy:

1. Children with NLD usually have excellent auditory memories. If homework is given to reinforce material learned in class, then it is entirely appropriate to reduce the amount expected of the child with NLD. Where examples are requested, experts like Sue Thompson (Thompson 1997) suggest that the NLDer do one for every ten that neurotypical children are required to complete.

2. Many children with NLD have extreme difficulties getting organized to begin their work, and spend inordinate amounts of time getting started. Some develop obsessive compulsive disorder (OCD) and enact rituals related to homework that delay the completion of work which they consider appropriate to hand in. For example, if they make a mistake on a page, some will not erase and feel compelled to start over. Others become frustrated if their columns are not straight, yet are caught in a vicious cycle because their disability renders them inherently unable to produce straight columns.

3. If homework assignments are written on the board, some children with NLD are unable to copy the assignment correctly due to visual-spatial difficulties. If they have a homework buddy, they can call or e-mail to verify the assignment. Unfortunately, some children with NLD have no idea that they have written down the assignment incorrectly and will persevere in trying to complete an assignment that is simply impossible to complete.

4.   Due to low self-esteem, some children with NLD refuse to ask for clarification even when they really do not know how to begin working on a homework assignment. They will look at the instructions for hours trying to make sense of something they do not understand rather than express their bewilderment to someone who might be able to help.

A proactive parent can prevent some of these homework pitfalls by anticipating what might happen, and by developing a system at the beginning of each school year for the systematic delivery of assignments in a homework notebook sent home regularly, or by e-mail or fax. There should also be a clearly articulated agreement among the teacher, student, and family members that if the homework is taking longer than an agreed-upon period of time, if the instructions seem unclear, or if the task seems inappropriate, then the parent and the NLDer have the right to bypass that assignment without penalty or recrimination.

Let's now look at the social, emotional, and behavioral components which can affect each stage of your child's schooling.

Preschool and kindergarten

During their early school years, most children who are ultimately diagnosed with NLD do not yet have an official name for the behaviors and learning styles which differentiate them from their peers. They do not usually look different, and since many relate exceptionally well to adults, their teachers often consider them intellectually precocious and delightful. But the careful observer will notice subtle differences in processing speed, in peer interaction, in fine motor dexterity, and in coordination. Those trained to evaluate language may begin to realize that the highly developed vocabulary used by some children with NLD rests on a foundation of precarious language pragmatics, or they may begin to suspect some difficulties with central auditory processing.

If you notice that your child has trouble with coordination, fine or gross motor activities, the preschool years are a good time for a full occupational therapy assessment and occupational therapy designed to help coordinate sensory information with motor activity. Not all children with sensory integration dysfunction have NLD, but many people with NLD have Sensory

Integration Dysfunction. By addressing this early observable symptom before other problems become apparent, it may be possible to alleviate the severity of things to come.

One three-year-old, as yet undiagnosed NLDer attended a loving pre-school where grandmotherly teachers held the children on their laps, sang songs, and told stories. A child could do nothing wrong. In fact, a child could do nothing, period. The teachers made all the arts and crafts projects, did all the cutting and pasting, and turned any artwork that wasn't profes-sional into confetti. In retrospect, I should probably have kept my child there until he was 16, just for the unconditional positive regard; but at the time, I was too naïve to see the value of decorating my refrigerator with artwork by 50-year-old matrons.

I switched him to a community center school which was taught by "real" teachers. There he was considered a brilliant eccentric. Of course he didn't like physical education; he was too cerebral. Why run around like a four-year-old when you can have a conversation with your teacher about different varieties of artichoke? And speaking of running around, why could we find no answers in the professional community when, at four years old, toilet training became for him a lost art? The psychologist we consulted said, "I feel as though there are two people in the room with me. One is a four-year-old boy, but the other is an 80-year-old man."

At five, our child never expressed a moment's regret as we prepared each morning for a year of pre-kindergarten. Although the teachers were intrigued by his occasional scholarly monologues, they assured his father and me that he was otherwise a "regular kid," who participated in group activities, went willingly to all specials, and seemed engaged in the generally happy business of being a five-year-old. What a surprise for all of us, then, when this happy and engaged preschooler decorated the walls of the boys' lavatory with his own feces. Since he had never before shown a predilection for interior design, we consulted his pediatrician.

"This is a symptom of nothing but rage," he stressed. "Something is infu-riating your child." We looked quizzically at the man who had been so helpful with our three older children. "Rage?" This was the sweetest, funniest, gentlest child of our four. I set out to research the possibilities of the totally unconscionable behavior which all of us hoped was the one-time expression of something trivial, with emphasis on the "one time."

I can't remember ever researching a more noxious topic. "...behaviors of severe trauma," I read, "such as soiling himself and smearing feces..." I conjured up a memory of this potential severely traumatized child curled up in a comfortable chair in his fleece pajamas. "Naah," I thought, "not trauma." After reading more than I had ever wanted to know, I found some information which made an interesting connection between sensory integration, toilet training, body sensations, and everyday functional activities.

Some children have trouble "reading" the body cues which tell them that they need to use the toilet. Others get so involved in the sensory stimulation of the "product" that smearing feces is not uncommon. The child may also be overwhelmed by the sensory environment of the toilet, with loud flushing noises, echoes, rushing water, and a chair with a big hole in it right over this water!

This child had displayed acute responses to sensory issues since infancy. In fact, he had once been so overcome by environmental stimuli that he had sought refuge in a dark closet. This was a child who would beg his mother to stop singing in the car (everyone's a critic!) or wiggle away from a hug as though it transmitted infectious disease. Preschool, which helped the family connect sensory issues to behavior, was the first stop on this child's journey to the ultimate diagnosis of NLD. It is also a *caveat* to parents – if you know that a diagnosis does not fit your child, keep exploring.

Kindergarten

Robert Fulghum may have learned everything he needed to know in kindergarten, but children with NLD definitely do not. They rarely master the actual hands-on kindergarten craft of cutting and pasting, although some are quite proficient at the computer skill of the same name by this age. They have inordinate trouble learning to perform a multistep procedure like going to their cubby, putting on a coat, and lining up near the door. When this project is complicated by winter's demand for boots, mittens, and hats, they can often be found in the coat room in a total state of decompensation. Teachers punish them for dawdling, peers ridicule them for awkwardness, and bus drivers or carpool parents scold them for tardiness. Just a few months into the first formal year of school, the incipient NLDer has learned a very important lesson: This is not going to be a whole lot of fun.

Although the feces incident remains the lowest point of preschool, it is almost eclipsed by the first teacher meeting with the soon-to-be-diagnosed NLDer's mother and his kindergarten teacher. Our family was living outside of the United States when our oldest child attended kindergarten, but the next two had availed themselves wholeheartedly of the program in our neighborhood school. I had never intervened in the choice of teachers, but something told me that the fourth little Rubinstien might benefit from the most structured kindergarten teacher available. After conducting clandestine research in the school's parking lot and hallways, I had a meeting with the principal, baked some highly caloric ethnic delights for the secretary, and volunteered for every school activity between the upcoming kindergarten year and my eightieth birthday. Then I suggested that it might be beneficial if my youngest were placed in a certain class, and, lo, it came to be.

Although I was familiar with this teacher's name and reputation (both good), none of my older children had ever been in her class. Feeling certain that the incident in the boys' bathroom was behind us, literally and figuratively, I was sure that I had entrusted my child to the best classroom with the most qualified teacher. The part of me that was really sure about that was quite pleased. The other part waited for a phone call and was reassured daily when none transpired. I looked forward to good news at the first parent–teacher conference in November. I arrived on time for the conference. Taking my yellow pad and pen in hand, I put a smile on my face, and promised myself to let the teacher do the talking.

And talk she did. Her words are forever engraved on my brain. They say an alcoholic never forgets the feeling of taking that first drink. Well, if I go completely senile and have only one neuron left to fire, that neuron will contain the feeling of that first conference. Pleasantries were exchanged. "Yeah, yeah," I thought. "Get on with it. Tell me about the little genius."

"Well," she began, "I really have no way to evaluate your son…"

"Of course not," I was thinking. "He's probably off the charts in everything you expect him to do in kindergarten."

Luckily, I stopped thinking in time to start listening and hear her say, "…because he has done nothing that I could possibly evaluate. He is simply a nonproductive lump."

"Just a minute," I remonstrated. "Do you know who I am?"

"I know exactly who you are, and I *am* talking about your son. When I say 'left,' he goes right. When I say 'sit,' he stands. When I give an assignment, he looks dazed and then asks questions about exactly the same things I told the class while I was giving the assignment. When we go to lunch, he heads for the gym. And as for gym, he has never once managed to get his sneakers on in time to participate in anything before the period ends. Once I sent him to the office to get a paper signed and I found him two hours later chatting with the librarian."

I didn't download the rest of this diatribe to my brain until about an hour later. I was still stuck on "nonproductive lump." I was sure you could sue a teacher for talking like that about a child. That was what I would do. I would sue her and get my son out of her toxic classroom. Obviously she didn't have the credentials to teach a child of his intellectual caliber. Just as I was planning the courtroom ploys, the next parent tapped me on the shoulder and said, "I think your fifteen minutes are up."

I needed no excuse to get out of there. I ran home to discuss this with my husband. Then I called my unsuspecting son into our room and asked him to tell us about Mrs. Broccolini (her name has been changed to protect me – I still gag when I confront it). He looked at us as if we had requested a 30-page report on lederhosen fashions in thirteenth-century Lichtenstein. "Who?" he said. Right about then I knew. Houston, we have a problem.

Kindergarten was off to a horrific start because both the teacher and I suffered from a lack of appropriate and organized information. I had asked for a structured teacher because I was aware of my child's inherent tendency to dawdle, to daydream, and to disregard multistep instructions. If I had described these characteristics to the teacher instead of stressing his superior cognitive abilities, she might have thought that I had a bit more contact with reality.

Nothing can excuse describing a child as a nonproductive lump, but those of us who have lived with children who have NLD without understanding what drives their behavior have felt similar frustration. It was equally inexcusable that, as a professional supervising this important transition from preschool to elementary school, she had not been taught to screen behaviors that might indicate neurological rather than behavioral origins. Together, unknowingly, we had removed all options for an environment that could have been nurturing, enlightening, and a positive beginning to the lower school years.

Before you send your child to kindergarten, recognize your child's deficits as intimately as you appreciate all assets. Share everything with the school's teachers and administrators. Begin advocating for accommodations that favor your child's unique learning and processing style from the very first day of school. Become an active volunteer in class and a well-known contributor to school activities. The only nonproductive lump in your child's classroom should be the stone that serves as a door stop, and even that, on occasion, can hold the door open to exciting adventure.

Elementary school

The elementary school years, from Grades One through Six, represent the cognitive crest of a typical NLDer's academic career. Most subjects in these grades play to the strengths of the NLD mind. They require no sophisticated analysis and depend on rote memory. Mathematics has not yet gone into functions demanding visualization and working memory, so NLDers are quite capable of learning the basics, although some have trouble with fractions – the original part to whole concept. History and language arts play into strengths for summarizing and retelling. Occasionally teachers will remind the NLDer to put a little more descriptive language into a book report or to show the work when displaying a math function, but there are usually no major academic problems in the early school years.

The only problems which may affect an NLDer in primary grades deal with special classes like physical education and art. Your child may have trouble complying with the art teacher's demands on certain projects. In physical education, the difficulties may be more complex. If you have not sought the advice of an occupational therapist until now, there is still time for effective intervention. Your child will probably suffer some frustration getting changed on time for gym and returning to class on time. Mine conveniently forgot his locker number and left a pair of gym shorts at school from December through June. Penicillin was discovered in a similar way, but we decided not to pursue the scientific possibilities in this particular experiment.

Unfortunately, the seeds for the social disasters which blossom in middle school are sown by fourth or fifth grade. Children have an instinct for zeroing in on those who are most vulnerable. Often it is the child who has NLD. Although they may have been awed by his or her astonishing memory and knowledge in third grade, the rudimentary behaviors of the prepubescent pack set in shortly thereafter and neurotypical kids follow tacit group decisions about which classmate to bully, tease, and ostracize.

If your child comes home unhappy or seems reluctant to discuss things that happened in school, try to clarify the situation to make sure that an academic assignment or a school activity has not placed too much stress on the neurological capabilities of your child. This is the time when you need to demand that the school make modifications to ensure your child's optimal participation. If there is too much homework, reduce the assignment. Help find a way to present new material gradually and gently so that there is a "shelf" prepared for it in the brain when the unit is introduced in class. Make sure that class trips or enrichment projects do not contain the classic pitfalls that affect children with NLD, making inappropriate demands on your child's sensorimotor, visual-spatial, or organizational capabilities.

The parents of elementary school children need to make sure that every assignment and activity is available in a format appropriate for their child, that each is modified for his or her highest level of capability, and that every child with a learning difference feels included and validated by his or her effort. To make matters even more complex, the parent must do all of this without making it obvious to the child's peers that such constant support is being given.

Parents of children with neurological disorders are like silent stage-hands. Between the acts, the stagehands rush behind the curtains to rear-range the sets and adjust anything that they anticipate might cause trouble. They dress in black so that they won't be obtrusive to theatergoers or actors. They analyze the strengths and weaknesses of each actor in rehearsal and know who has a tendency to bump into a chair or who will scramble off irresponsibly toward the wrong side of the stage. Then they wait in the wings to make sure that the actors have whatever they need to perform opti-mally. If a prop is missing or inappropriate, they scramble silently to make a replacement or adjustment. They consider the best shows to be those in which nobody notices anything that they do. Although they rarely receive applause, everyone involved with the performance knows that the show could never go on without their constant, steady vigilance.

For NLDers in elementary school, everyone working backstage helps determine whether the show will be a roaring success or a dismal flop. If you can raise the awareness of every teacher, administrator, and staff member in the school, your child has the potential to be a star. Make sure that key people have information about conferences, speakers, and publications which deal with NLD and related issues. Maintain a gentle, supportive presence in school by offering to volunteer at school events. Chaperone trips and help the teacher with any modifications related to your child. There may be days when you want to go in and scream until the rafters shake. Instead, try therapy, transcendental meditation, or some really fine chocolate. In the long run, saving your self-respect will result in bigger and better pay-offs for your child.

Middle school

In middle school, the boys turn into hormones on feet and the girls recreate divisive systems of class and privilege that most democratic nations have spent centuries trying to destroy. Children with NLD are usually literal, justice-oriented, fair-minded, and unable to read nonverbal signals. Although NLD does not affect their physical maturation in any way, their awareness of themselves as sexual/social beings usually awakens much later than the peer norm. In other words, they haven't got a single game piece for playing on the middle school social board. If that weren't enough to alienate them from their classmates, changes in the middle school academic program also complicate matters for the typical NLDer.

Most primary schools teach children in inclusive classrooms except for physical education and special classes like music and art. But in middle school, most children move from teacher to teacher, making it necessary to find classrooms all over the school building in what may only be a short time allowed between bells. NLDers can become unsettled by the need to collect their belongings, navigate their way to a new location, re-establish themselves in a new site, and be ready to absorb totally different subject matter, all within the passing time of three to five minutes. Those lucky enough to make it intact are then faced with the cruelest challenge of middle school – the need to recruit a whole new set of learning skills from their most neurologically deficient areas.

In middle school, talents for rote memory or spelling are things of the past. By this level of education, a student is expected to use interhemispheric skills, such as analysis, conceptualization, insight, and imagination. These processes, even for NLDers who can achieve them, can be painfully slow. Sometimes, during class assignments, others will finish their work before the NLDer has even developed a viable plan of action. Parents and teachers should be careful to grant extended time and never to ridicule NLDers to taking more time to process and plan. There is a very delicate balance between empowering the NLDer to develop academic coping skills or leaving the middle schooler with NLD to conclude that he or she is less capable than most of his or her classmates.

Non-structured times, such as lunch, recess, and times between class, can be periods of brutal confrontation between children with NLD and their neurotypical peers. Many choose simply to isolate, but others expose them-selves to taunting and bullying with a painful combination of optimism and resilience. Some schools offer interventions such as social skills groups and lunch buddies, but the harsh reality is that neurotypical children of middle school age rarely have enough of a social conscience to include children with even the slightest difference in their exclusive circles. They also do not have the maturity or discrimination to appreciate the value of a different perspective. The peer group is the main defense against the fears and changes they themselves are confronting daily. Opening it to someone who doesn't meet their predefined description of "cool" leaves them with the lin-gering possibility that they themselves might also be the slightest bit uncool. The neurotypical preadolescent would rather die than willingly accept that consequence. For this reason, ostracism of someone different, which will (one hopes) be recognized as a moral wrong in later life, is accepted as a foundation of preadolescent group behavior.

Problems for middle school NLDers are exacerbated by their growing confidence in the "rightness" of things they have learned, their increasing difficulty in recognizing that gray areas truly do exist between the polarities of black and white, and their increasing inability to understand whether or not to belabor a point. One parent discussed how her child totally alienated a teacher by trying to correct an error that no one else in class had noticed. A classroom quiz had asked students how many days it takes the moon to spin through its full cycle, and everyone else in the class received full credit for writing 28 days, the answer the teacher had expected.

The NLDer, however, correct in both literal and scientific domains, wrote, "The moon doesn't spin," and received no credit for his answer. A child with more political savvy might approach the teacher after class to explain that he had understood what the teacher was going for, but that technically, the moon's rotation around the earth should not be classified as spinning. Instead, a child with NLD characteristically chooses to begin this elucidation in class, endearing himself neither to his peers nor to the typical teacher. Even adults with NLD find it difficult to explain why the need to clarify supersedes social stratification. "I just like to be right," one explains.

So what happens to middle school NLDers who are not cool, and who confront complex cognitive difficulties? Most look for ways to cope emotionally. Some find healthy compensations, and others act out, become depressed, or adopt at-risk behaviors. This is an extremely important time for parents to remember that NLDers respond best when supported and not confronted. If you can see that your middle schooler is in trouble, find a competent professional to help you assess the situation on all levels – academic, social, and emotional/behavioral. Sometimes medication can help, sometimes it is useless, and in the worst cases, it exacerbates the problem. Sometimes an exercise program can work wonders, at other times it can create resentment. And sometimes, there is simply no other treatment but chocolate. The latter should be ingested in moderation. By parents.

There is only one truly positive thing to say about middle school. It is usually the shortest division in a school system. Before you have time to buy stock in the Kleenex corporation, the kids are off to high school and a whole new set of challenges.

High school

By the time children with NLD get to high school, most have been diagnosed with some sort of learning disorder, even if it hasn't exactly been defined as NLD. Some are relieved to learn that there is a reason for their learning differences; some are angry that they experience difficulty with tasks that seem easy for others. Still another group, many NLDers among them, refuse to acknowledge that there is anything different or unusual about the way they learn or assess information.

If high school is larger, less personal, and more regimented than the smaller, neighborhood-based elementary and middle schools, your child's transition could be difficult. You should spend time with a transition team to make sure that all academic and emotional supports are in place. You should make sure that all people who will have an impact on your child's daily life at school know about the syndrome of NLD and understand its complex ramifications. Take your child to the school several times before the academic year begins to guarantee that everything will be familiar and that he or she can develop a general sense of how to get from home room to the gym, from music to the cafeteria, and from anywhere in school to the nurse's office. Be nosy. Ask your child what feels good and what feels uncomfortable about the high school. Don't accept a grunt for an answer, although that is the typical mode of communication for adolescents.

If you are sending your child to a small independent school, make sure that you know exactly what the school philosophy is on social interaction. I saw a brilliant, handsome young man in my office who had spent three years as a student at one of New England's best-known independent schools. Teachers loved him for his insightful classroom participation, his caring manner, and his true commitment to learning. For some reason, however, his classmates had decided to completely exclude him from all social circles on campus.

Although administrators and faculty members had been informed of this problem and had discussed it with the student and his parents, they were unable to break the social code that tacitly allowed regimented bullying. After three years, this young man came to see me about changing schools and literally wept in my office. When I asked him what he was good at, he answered, "I could have told you lots of things three years ago, but now I don't even know what to say."

Back in public school as a high school senior, he is active in school clubs, athletics, takes advanced courses, and is enrolled in two courses at a nearby university. He has plenty to say when asked what he is good at. More important, he says it with a smile. This boy fell victim to a school culture which couldn't and wouldn't do anything to uproot its toxic traditions. Make sure you speak to parents, students, and alumni before you choose a school.

If you are looking at an independent residential school, the caveats increase geometrically. Since your child will be spending 24 hours a day in a living and learning environment away from his or her family, make sure that he or she is living and learning to be healthy and happy, not diseased and depressed. In addition to your own investigation, it is wise to enlist the help of a professional educational consultant. Consultants visit schools regularly and know exactly what is going on not only during the school day, but during unscheduled time and after lights out. My child had a positive life-altering experience in a small independent residential school. The environment made room for his quirks while providing a framework of non-negotiables that made him ready to confront real-world requirements. However, for each success I celebrate, I see many who were not as lucky. The key to finding the right school is to know your child's needs, and to investigate before you act.

Post-secondary placements and college

Not everyone should attend college. This statement is as true for neurotypicals as it is for people with NLD. The consideration of options for late adolescent and adult life is based on a multivariate analysis of factors, ranging from intellectual ability, practical ability, capacity to persevere, level of determination, courage, to immeasurable factors like heart, grit, personality, and resilience. Intelligence is only a small factor in the equation. We have all heard of mad geniuses who spent their lives isolated from society. Before the NLDer considers transitioning to independent living and learning, global capabilities must be carefully assessed.

Organizational skills are probably the most important competencies for managing an independent life. Can the young adult with NLD control the basics of daily living without active hands-on assistance from a parent or family member? If so, it might be possible to live independently at college.

Second, cognitive abilities must be assessed. There is a wide range of intellectual abilities addressed at colleges and universities throughout the world, but understanding of the unique perspective of a student with NLD is far more important than the level of cerebral stimulation. Does the college under consideration offer support for students with different learning styles? If so, it might be a good choice.

Because no person can live a healthy adult life without some sort of interpersonal interaction, the social situation is a critical part of the transition decision. What distinguishes the student mix at the school being considered? Is it exclusionary, with definite "in" and "out" groups, or does the school pride itself on being a place where all types of people can learn and live together? If diversity is celebrated, NLDers may find themselves able to be comfortably ensconced.

It is important to remember that transitions cause anxiety for NLDers, whether they are going to preschool or college. The level of this anxiety, and the measure of disability it creates, will determine how successful a young adult with NLD can be in peer society beyond high school. If continuing support and appropriate resources have bolstered self-esteem and initiative throughout the school years, there is reason to hope that the NLDer will encounter success as he or she searches for a meaningful way in the world.

We must never forget that in school, children with NLD can face a non-stop barrage of performance demands from peers and authority figures. I have studied NLD in scholarly and personal venues for more than a decade. Everything I have learned leads me to believe that the child with this diagnosis who wakes up day after day and enters a mainstream school without accommodations gives testament to the indomitable nature of the human spirit. I also believe that for some of our children, attending school can feel like ingesting a steady diet of emotional abuse. It is high time that we force our schools to stop abusing children with NLD. The recommendations below, taken from suggestions by parents, educators, and healthcare providers, represent an idealized, but viable, list of ways in which educators could make our schools safe and productive for children with NLD.

Don't rest until all of these recommendations are in place at your child's school.

For teachers and administrators

1. Approach our kids without prejudice. Understand that if they're having a problem, it's probably neurological in origin and not a show of oppositional behavior.

2. Please learn to read each child's signs of happiness and distress. Children with NLD suffer from profound anxiety. If you can

learn to recognize stress points and relieve them with simple explanations or alternate activities, you could make your child much happier and more productive.

3. Please teach children with NLD a variety of learning strategies so that they become independent learners.

4. Please design NLD-friendly problem pages and homework sheets. Some children with visual-spatial problems are absolutely overwhelmed when they see a page full of math problems and will never be able to get started on that work. But if you show them how to fold the page so that only one problem is showing, they can focus and begin to work. Most NLDers are willing and able to do the work, but when an assignment sheet is visually cluttered, it is inaccessible and, for that reason, undoable.

5. Please make sure that every child with NLD has an extra set of books to keep at home, so that he or she won't have to worry about scrambling to get everything ready during the last hectic moments of school.

6. Please ask verbally for homework each time an assignment is due. NLDers don't remember to put their work into a homework file without daily oral reminders. Some don't even remember that they have done their homework if not specifically reminded.

7. When abstract concepts must be used, remember to provide additional verbal information that breaks down and explains the abstract idea in detail.

8. Remember that most children with NLD can't understand metaphors, emotional nuances, multiple levels of meanings, and relationship issues unless you explain them simply and patiently.

9. Don't confuse good reading skills with good reading comprehension.

10.   Make children with NLD feel comfortable about asking for clarification. Give them the skills to verbalize what it is they don't understand and help them believe that you are willing to give them the time and consideration they require.

11.   Don't expect children with NLD to give immediate responses. They need time to process information. Develop systems that help them feel comfortable and save face while taking time to formulate answers in class. For example, instead of just calling on a student and expecting an answer right away, you could say, "Javier, I would love to hear what you have to say about the rotation of the moon. Why don't you think about it while we finish this topic and then we can share some of your ideas?"

12.   Please read each NLDer's education plan before the school year starts. NLD is very different from the language-based learning disabilities with which you might be more familiar. Each day that you treat the NLDer inappropriately could cause days of setbacks, anxiety, and distress.

13.   If you read a book about NLD, and my child does not react according to the description, don't assume that he or she has been misdiagnosed. There is no single profile for NLD. If my child is displaying a certain behavior, it is probably a behavior which is one of the complex ramifications of this syndrome.

14.   Children with NLD are uncompromisingly literal. This is not an attempt to be "wise" or rude. It is the manifestation of a neurological disorder.

And finally, most important,

15.   Accept my child as he or she is. Take this child as far as you can during your time together. Approach the deficits with patience, the assets with commendation, and the anxieties with compassion. Perhaps one day you will be lucky enough to have a child with NLD whom you will love as much as we love ours.

Key points

1.   For children with NLD, attending school with teachers and administrators who do not understand their academic, social, and emotional needs can be the most difficult and frustrating sustained experience they face in their lives.

2.   NLD is considered a learning disability for the following reasons:

     ○   people with NLD find new learning difficult

     ○   they over-rely on previously learned information

     ○   their lack of adaptability causes some deficiencies in learning

     ○   they can't integrate learned information with applications in process.

3.   Because schools are more aware of language-based learning differences than they are of NLD, parents of NLDers must become full-time advocates, monitoring not only academics but also attitudes. To help the child with NLD adjust to the world, every point of contact with that world must be explained.

4.   The academic, social, and emotional needs of NLDers change as they mature. At all levels of schooling, and even as they transition to post-secondary programs or independent living, we must guarantee that educators approach our children with a variety of strategies for becoming confident and capable learners.

Chapter Seven
Chow and How

Do you remember when Ward and June sat down to dinner with Wally and the Beav? June always wore a crisp apron and a string of pearls. Ward had a suit on, of course, and the boys always looked impeccable despite the fact that they had allegedly spent the day at school and the afternoon "playing" in the backyard. "Mom," Wally would ask politely, "could you please pass the potatoes?" "Of course, dear," June would respond glowingly as her culinary efforts were rewarded.

Sophisticated teenage Wally, not a vowel out of place on his letter sweater, and even the clueless Beav, perhaps the earliest nationally broadcast prototype for NLD behavior, displayed their irreproachable table manners until they had consumed their dessert and asked to be excused. It wasn't until Steven Spielberg allowed Drew Barrymore to call her brother "Penisbreath" during breakfast in *ET* that the media brought us a more realistic notion of the American family at mealtime.

In truth, nothing short of *Alien* could ever prepare us for the issues that some children with NLD can develop around food, family interaction, and table manners. Food and family gatherings seem to combine to bring out all the latent ineptitudes and anxieties that lurk inside the child with NLD. For someone with sensorimotor problems, coordinating

Western utensils is as difficult as having Edward Scissorhands use chopsticks.

Consider the typical family dinner. Mom and Dad, though each innately capable of secret slurping, generally display socially acceptable dining habits in public. Eight-year-old Hortense and five-year-old Horton are eating at age-appropriate levels of delicacy. But Heywood, an eleven-year-old with NLD, seems unaware of the physical relationship between his plate, his food, and his mouth. His fork takes an astonishingly convoluted trajectory from plate to mouth, dripping splotches of variegated foodstuffs on the tablecloth like Jackson Pollack. He is always distracted by other things when he is eating and pays no attention to how he is eating unless he is constantly reminded. He also has a tendency to lean back in his chair at mealtime so that the kitchen chairs, not originally contemporary in shape, are now bizarrely contorted from all the leaning.

Although this family had envisioned erudite conversations about culture and philosophy over dinner, most of their evenings sound like this:

- "Hey, would you stop dripping chili sauce all over the chocolate chip cookies?"

- "Hey, would you sit up straight? That's the second chair I've replaced this year. Soon I'll have to get a whole new kitchen set."

- "Hey, would you get your head out of the pasta, or are you taking scuba lessons?"

When Heywood comes back to earth from his state of distraction, he smiles and wipes his hands on his pants while his little brother looks on with undying approval. His sister contracts her entire face like a goldfish sucking a lemon and says, "Eeeuw!" A casual observer might assume that a rude, manipulative, oppositional child was controlling and enslaving a family undeserving of such treatment. But actually, the child with NLD is neither rude nor oppositional. Most likely, his or her behaviors are based in neurobiological origins that manifest as:

- inappropriate interpersonal behaviors stemming from misinterpretation of social cues

- sensory reactions related to taste, texture, or temperature of foods

- psychomotor or tactile/spatial deficits related to difficulty with handling utensils effectively.

By viewing the child with NLD as a child who *cannot* rather than a child who *will not*, we change our perspective from disgust to discussed. Since auditory and verbal skills are often the greatest asset of a child with NLD, the more we discuss a behavior and its consequences, the greater the likelihood of helping a child understand how to remediate inappropriate behavior.

But, if we are discussing dinner for children with NLD, we have arrived at the table far too quickly. There is much to be considered before sitting down to eat. If you prethink the situation, a strategy that is helpful for every aspect of life with NLD, you can prevent many post-prandial pitfalls and make dinnertime more of a delight than a disaster.

For many reasons, kids with NLD have trouble sitting still. Their difficulties with balance, and their need for sensory – usually proprioceptive – stimulation, makes it difficult for them to sit quietly in the type of straight-backed chair traditionally used by families in Western cultures at mealtimes. (Most kids with NLD also lean back as far as they can in any car seat or movie seat.) We have actually had to replace our kitchen chairs twice over a period of ten years because they couldn't take the unnatural angles that were demanded of them during dinner. Children who have NLD in some relaxed cultures where they eat dinner reclining on pillows in the seraglio, or where only the natural God-given utensils are used, are probably thought to have excellent table manners. But for most of us in the Western hemisphere, knife, fork, spoon, chair, and family interaction can present daunting challenges to kids with NLD.

If you have the luxury of choosing the style of furniture where your family will share most meals with your NLDer, think sturdy, solid, and immovable. Built-in booths are terrific, although they're seldom found outside of diners, and few families establish permanent residence in diners. As a second choice, sturdy, broad-bottomed chairs that don't lend themselves to spindle-spinning can be a great comfort to a child who is always trying to find a comfortable balance. You should also check that tables pass the tip-top test before coming home from the store, making sure that they don't tip over when pressure is applied to one side or another or when a teenager decides to take a nap with most of his upper body resting on the tabletop.

Many families have assigned seats at dinner, some random seating, and others merely fight for front seat or back. But if your family gathers regularly around a table indoors for mealtime, it's a good idea to assign seats. Place your NLDer next to a person who can give quiet reinforcement and support and far from anyone who might voice offense at a random dribble.

Though many families watch television at mealtime – "I just need to catch up on the news" – this is generally not a great idea. Divisive even in the best of situations, it just adds another component which could lead to sensory overload for your NLDer, who has enough to concentrate on just thinking about cutting the meat.

Lovely, flickering scented candles are wonderful for romantic dinners, but for family dinners with your NLDer, they could be the straws that break the camel's back. Find out what level of light is most comfortable for your child with NLD, and use that setting in the kitchen or dining room while eating. Some kids with NLD are very uncomfortable with bright light, and others find it difficult to see what they're doing if the lights are too dim. There's a happy medium somewhere – just be aware that you need to discern what it is.

Setting the table is a task you can definitely do with your NLDer – from an early age. As we all know, there are fairly traditional expectations for flatware placement in our society. It might even help if you take out a book from the library showing your child how a table is set, so that he or she doesn't think you made up the rules to be arbitrary. The prepared job cards that we discussed in Chapter 4 are excellent ways to secure consistency and prevent creativity in areas where the rules are fairly conventional. Another good way to engage cooperation is by saying that someday, when your children are visiting friends, they may be asked to set the table. It's a good functional, transferable skill. Unfortunately, as your NLDer will probably point out to you, it's not particularly useful in certain remote African and Asian cultures. If your family eats by dipping your fingers or palm leaves into a central bowl, you can save yourself this entire non-negotiable step.

Most families who have children with NLD learn fairly quickly that white linen tablecloths are best suited for homes of the rich, famous, and neurotypical. I wish I had taped the conversation I once had with my son

about napkins. Usually we use paper napkins, which he considers abomina-
ble because they destroy the environment. I basically agree with him, so
occasionally we use cloth napkins (especially on *bona fide* occasions, like
birthdays, holidays, and days when no one has been suspended from
school). I had assumed that on those nights he would not need reminding to
use the napkin instead of his pants, but then I faced this logic: "Mom, you
have to wash my pants, anyway, but if I don't use the napkin, I'm actually
saving you work." Well, my fellow exasperated diners, I won this case with
the following argument (after many rebuttals): "Yes, but napkins are small
squares of material designed specifically for messy hands and mouths, and
are usually made of material which washes easily and well, while pants
contain other fibers not necessarily designed to absorb grease or spaghetti
sauce. They may require more washings and cause even more unnatural
chemicals to be added to the eco-system."

I have always been a great fan of swipe 'em and wipe 'em placemats,
although my NLDer has exceeded the boundaries of his placemat with
mealtime residue on more than one occasion. Though far from elegant,
these plastic table savers have allowed my oak tabletop to remain fairly serviceable for more than twenty years. This may not sound like an astonishing
achievement for a solid chunk of wood that probably served its original tree
for centuries, but children with NLD have a way of being very hard on per-
ishable goods. This is not through acts of willful destruction. In most cases,
they are simply unaware of the effect of their bodies in space. In the case of
my child, his body grew to be six feet and four inches tall, and engaged itself
in battles with our kitchen table and chairs on many occasions. At this point,
I would say that they are equally matched. Both sides bear a few scars, but
are still fully functional.

Now that we have clarified where dinner will be served, it's time to
discuss what to serve. There is no predictable listing of what children with
NLD will eat, but it is fairly predictable to assume that their tastes will be
categorical and quirky. Many parents of younger kids with NLD report that
their offspring stick faithfully to the "white diet" for years. This colorless
cuisine is not really a chromatic comment, but rather a textural preference
based on foods that are safe, smooth, and predictable.

For many children with NLD, hypotonia, oral defensiveness, and
anxiety can interact with eating and swallowing, so foods like simple pasta,

rice pudding, yogurt, and white bread are safe and harbor no hidden surprises. They are also available at most homes and restaurants. This choice of
diet is so common to kids with NLD that it is almost a diagnostic predictor.
When I recently met new school placement clients at a restaurant for the first
interview, I was surprised to see their sixteen-year-old son order angel hair
pasta with butter and parmesan cheese. Before we had even begun our conversation, I suspected and later confirmed the diagnosis of NLD.

Other NLDers are open to multicolored meals, but refuse certain
textures. "I don't do soup" was a refrain for years in my house, from a child
who was adventurous enough to list the artichoke as his favorite food in a
kindergarten "All About Me" report.

"Please try this," I would whine. After all, I sprang from generations of
Jewish mothers who were convinced great harm could come to children
who did not ingest untold quantities of chicken soup. "Are you sure you
don't want a fluffy matzo ball in just enough broth to keep it hydrated?" I
cajoled.

But suddenly I saw the light. For someone with NLD who might have
trouble with fine motor coordination, it was complicated to bring a slithery
substance on a spoon from the table to the mouth. Soup, or more literally
porridge, as Goldilocks taught us all, could be uncomfortably hot or
unpleasantly cold. Even if it found its way to the mouth without incident, if
it didn't turn out to be "just right," it was as difficult to return to its place of
origin as it had been to transport on its original journey. Despite my ethnic
indoctrination, I had never read in a nutritional journal or sensationalist
tabloid that a child had died from lack of soup. So, I began to allow my child
to choose the foods and textures he wanted to eat, and mealtime became a
truce rather than a travesty. Today my son enjoys all kinds of soup from miso
to mushroom. Confident in his control over spoon, bowl, texture, and temperature, he makes up for his years of souplessness with grace and gusto.

Parents often worry that kids who eat such a lackluster diet will suffer
from nutritional deficiencies and they may in fact be correct. Although kids
with NLD usually don't enjoy swallowing pills, there are many types of
vitamin supplements that can keep them healthy and productive through
the growing years, some of which can be camouflaged in even the whitest of
meals. If subterfuge doesn't seem like a viable option, find a vitamin regimen
and make it non-negotiable. Children with NLD are often very concerned

about their health. If they understand the reasons for taking vitamin supplements, they can be surprisingly compliant.

Since we can assume that NLD appears in every culture the world over, there are probably young children with NLD who eat happily and unremarkably out of a common bowl. Others, I'm sure, join their parents and siblings in dipping wedges of fresh warm bread into the simple offerings spread out before them. But most of us in Western cultures expect our children to master the use of knife, fork, and spoon and to understand the intricacies of a dinner plate, drinking glass, and napkin before entering first grade. It's true that Europeans think Americans eat backwards and Americans wonder why such relatively nonaggressive people always have their knives poised for attack, but except for a few cross-cultural quirks, there is a Western code of rules for appropriate eating known as "table manners."

For two reasons, children with NLD find these rules very difficult to accept. First, they are often illogical, and children with NLD are programmed to combat illogical rules with endless questions and resolute resistance. I have never been able to answer why we set the table with the fork at the left hand. After all, most Americans do eat with the fork in their right hand. In fact, when you sit at a table grudgingly set by my son, that is where you will find your fork, the survivor of a battle from which I chose to retreat (I mentioned this in Chapter 4). Second, due to a combination of visual-spatial, tactile, and psychomotor difficulties, many children with NLD find it difficult to hold and handle utensils as most neurotypical people do. They can often be seen stabbing their food with their forks at uncommon angles, or trying to saw through seemingly tractable portions of meat or fish with their knives held at right angles to many the recalcitrant filet.

What may be good for a laugh at home, however, can create serious problems for children with NLD as they enter society at large. In order to avoid teasing and ostracism, children need to know how to eat respectably at school, in restaurants, and at the homes of others. This is another one of the non-negotiable elements of raising children who have trouble reading nonverbal cues that demands endless patience and practice. If you haven't prepared your child to feel comfortable performing one of the most basic life behaviors without being ridiculed, then you have not completed your job as the parent of a child with NLD. Back to the table, then, and put your napkin on your lap.

When the peas stop being projectiles, it might be time to try dinner in a restaurant. Most families with young children rarely get the opportunity to enjoy them, but there are actually establishments other than your vehicle where you can enjoy a meal away from home. Most people I know have an automatic default that answers "Reservations" when asked "What would you like for dinner?" Children with NLD, however, often prefer the safety of home to the uncharted territory of a restaurant. They activate a list of anxieties when they think about eating unfamiliar things, not finding anything they like on the menu, not knowing where the bathroom is, getting orange juice with all those awful little pieces in it, or even having to sit next to Mom in a booth instead of across from her at a table. These children are rarely spontaneous and cannot just hop into the car on the spur of the moment for an impromptu meal out. Until you have identified some places and menu items that are safe and predictable, eating out takes a lot of preloading.

First, make sure you choose a restaurant which serves food your child likes. Someone who hasn't ventured beyond anything spicier than tapioca pudding will probably not be very happy in Harry's House of Heat. Get a copy of the menu ahead of time and go over things your child might like to order. Explain what some of the things on the menu are. If the drinks on the menu look "funny," bring along a supply of whatever your child likes. Sometimes even very big babies need their bottles. If your child decides to order only an appetizer and dessert, just smile and go along with it. If your child orders a meal and doesn't eat it, pack it up and save it for lunch, siblings, Fido, or the garbage disposal. Your goal is to make the experience a pleasant one, not to have a fully integrated nutritional encounter.

When my NLDer was younger, he figured out an astute system for getting meals that he considered excellent at whatever restaurant he visited. Since he lives in a world that is very black and white, he decided that what was expensive must be good and what was cheap must be bad. Whenever we went to a "grown-up" restaurant, he simply ordered the most expensive item on the menu in each category. We never really knew if he liked what he ordered, but he was always convinced he had the best meal in the house. Today he is very interested in natural, organic, and healthy foods, so he has different criteria, but he still reads the menu carefully looking for "the best."

In a restaurant, as at home, table manners should be non-negotiable. But since your children can't ask to be excused unless they came in separate cars, you will have to determine the optimal length of your restaurant experience. As the meal winds down, it is extremely important to know when it is time to go home. Although at one point, this will become patently clear, the sophisticated parent should be able to recognize departure time a few moments before it becomes apparent to all of the other diners. Explain to your child that you may have to wait a few minutes, but ask for the bill and get ready to leave. Even if you were planning to order a cup of coffee, you probably wouldn't enjoy it.

Tolerance is a very clear-cut commodity for children with NLD. They either have it or they do not. When they don't, it's best not to broadcast that in a public place. As kids with NLD become adults with NLD, they learn, like the rest of us, that there are certain situations that can't be changed instantaneously. They learn to have more control over their emotions and their moods. But having already tested the reserves of your children with NLD by changing their routine and eating out, it's best not to push any other buttons. Buy a fancy coffeepot and enjoy a cappuccino at home.

So, why is dining, with all the complicated "do's and don'ts," such an issue anyway? Don't our kids have enough to learn without preparing to dine with royalty? It's an issue because, as parents, it's our job to educate, socialize, and normalize our children so that they can interact with neurotypical society and not seem inappropriate. Once in a while, you can dismiss your NLD kids early from the table or let them eat a meal sprawled all over the couch in the family room. But before you let them break the rules, make sure they know what the rules are. Like any creative progress, it's frustrating in the incipient stages, but when you uncover the masterpiece, it's more than worth the effort.

Key points

1.   Teaching table manners is a non-negotiable parental responsibility. Make sure that your child is capable of eating in public without causing a spectacle and without feeling uncomfortable. Insist that basic rules of gracious dining be followed at home so that they become almost intuitive when out in public.

2. Optimize your family dining – from furniture to flatware – for your NLDer's comfort. Don't make the path from appetizer to dessert an obstacle course. Observe your NLDer to learn what foods are preferred, what chairs are most comfortable, what utensils are easiest to handle.

3. Introduce restaurant experiences with patience and tolerance. The days of delicate dining with snowy linen and flickering flames must be tabled for a time. Until you introduce NLDers to the world of restaurant dining, you may never truly understand the meaning of fast food. Nevertheless, the introduction of new food-related experiences is another way to expand the experiential and sensory world of children with NLD.

4. No one has ever died from not eating soup.

Chapter Eight
Clothing

NLD is probably the only learning disability that comes with a uniform. Among the carefully calculated clones in full peer regalia stands a child wearing supple sweat pants with an elastic waistband. The accompanying solid color tee shirt is well-worn and washed into terminal softness. You may notice that the hem or neckband shows signs of having been absent-mindedly chewed or stretched into the shape of an abstract art-form. Completing the look is a pair of Velcro sneakers or laceless shoes, neither conforming to the latest standards of footwear fashion. At this moment, you are observing one of two probable social phenomena. Either you are watching a neophyte Method actor prepare for the middle school production of Oscar in *The Odd Couple*, or you are seeing a young person with NLD model the ideal ensemble to counteract his disorder of sensory integration.

The neurological deficits that define NLD influence sensorimotor capabilities in varying degrees. For many children, clothing can assuage or exacerbate motoric reactions, tactile defensiveness, temperature awareness, and fine motor coordination. Some garments, like bulky jackets or sportrelated gear, can even affect vestibular responsiveness in a child with NLD. As with every other aspect of this elusive syndrome, reactions to the issue of clothing vary according to the unique profile of the individual NLDer. However, most NLDers clearly have issues related to this essential component of daily life. The problem is so pervasive that, despite the availability of research to confirm my theory, I would assume that neuropsychologists investigating the populations of nudist colonies would probably find a large proportion of "nature lovers" with NLD, happily divested of clothing with itchy labels, bothersome fabrics, and troublesome closures.

By the age of six, a neurotypical child can suppress reflexive responses to touch situations (Kranowitz 1998). In other words, a child who wants to concentrate on making a snowman can ignore the fact that his warm woolen hat might be getting a little waterlogged or itchy. Similarly, neurotypical children of this age can button and zip competently. But children with problems in sensory integration don't receive appropriate messages from their brains. They may be hyper-responsive and take in so much sensory information that they overload, or they may be hypo-responsive and receive sensations which are less intense than normal. Others suffer from disorganized or inefficient processing of sensory data, or a combination of hypo- and hypersensitivity.

The most important thing for a parent to understand is that when the sensory neurons do not send efficient messages to the central nervous system, it is impossible for the child to react with correct behavioral responses. Your child's seemingly idiosyncratic reactions are not volitional or manipulative. In most cases, the child with NLD who displays sensory aversion or an inappropriate response to stimuli is simply responding to neurologically initiated messages which he or she cannot control.

For parents of children and teenagers with NLD, the challenge is to help them learn to dress in a way which will keep them comfortable enough to focus on other life tasks while looking acceptable enough to fit into the mainstream – even at its margins – and to avoid the ridicule and ostracism of their peers. If you need help in teaching the actual physical process of dressing, find an occupational therapist who makes your child feel comfortable and competent. Once the mechanics are accomplished, it is time for parents to learn about the complex emotional and behavioral relationship of children with NLD and their clothes.

I have never really understood the etymology of the phrase "hand-me-downs," but I have always enjoyed the bounty it represents. As a first-born, I rarely had the opportunity of wearing anyone else's clothing, but when I found my cousin's university blazer hanging in Aunt Rose's closet twenty years after Sally's graduation, I was delighted to wear it. The fact that Sally was uncommonly petite and I ultimately reached a height suitable for women's basketball concluded this relationship before I was ten years old, but I still remember the soft brown corduroy and the magical appeal of my older cousin's grown-up garb. I also received my first two-wheel bicycle through this benevolent system. All the cousins on my father's side learned to ride on a little, brown 18-inch bicycle that traveled from town to town to whatever cousin was ready to be liberated from training wheels.

Since I had such fond memories of this practical practice, it seemed only natural that my three sons should be delighted to wait patiently as things were passed down from sibling to sibling. The jeans that survived whatever it is that boys do to destroy a fabric that is allegedly the strongest ever designed for clothing, only got better and better with each incarnation. By the time they reached my third son, the son with NLD, they were as soft as fleece, and worn, shredded, or discolored in just the right places. I had already noticed that my children, like most individuals, had different clothing personalities. The oldest was a fashion plate, enjoying the sartorial superabundance that mothers often impose on their first-borns. The second son would have been happy to own one pair of pants and one tee-shirt, but agreed grudgingly to wear what he had to on non-negotiable occasions if given free rein within administrative limitations for school. Notably, in his early twenties, he wore the same tee-shirt for more than a year, although by then he was interested enough in interpersonal relationships to wash it frequently. Son number three, however, rewrote Rubinstien's Rules of Raiment.

"Hey, come try these on. I think you're ready to fit into this box of pants from the boys." Despite my truly upbeat attitude and purposely exaggerated facial expressions of delight, this was never a great attraction. Trying on clothes meant bending, buckling, zipping, pulling, and buttoning. Usually I resorted to some sort of bribery. When he was age three or four, I helped him try on a pair or two to see if the size was right and then just hovered surreptitiously to see if he needed assistance dressing in the morning. By the time he was five, however, this child had more categories for triage than the head nurse in an emergency room.

"Too waxy. Ouch – that pair buttons right where my bellybutton needs to breathe. Moooom – that fabric doesn't bend. Eeeeuw – slimy! Did you forget? I don't do stripes. Too itchy." The categories were endless. After years of trying to recycle, I finally realized that this child's clothing would have to be purchased for him, with him, and by him. It was impossible to argue or convince him, because his categories were not established by reason, but rather dictated by neurophysiology. If his neurology had directed him to wear nothing but a snakeskin vest and a marabou boa, I certainly would have started on a serious course of desensitization therapy. But making allowances for comfortable fasteners and fabrics seemed like a relatively small concession for a child who was already contending with multiple issues in the neurotypical world.

Whatever their preference, make sure that you help your NLDers comply with their needs in an understanding way. Never make fun of a dress style that is precipitated by neurological need. On the contrary, compliment your children when they are neatly dressed (try to catch them early in the day!) and help them feel attractive and appropriate.

Even though most NLDers are unaffected by fashion fads, it's helpful to make sure that they do not dress more than a few standard deviations outside of popular peer culture. Even though they may wear only one color and one fabric, you can at least guide them toward clothes in that color and fabric which are vaguely reminiscent of the styles worn by their peers. When they are old enough to decide that they are consciously flaunting fashion, that's fine. When they are young enough to need assistance buying clothes, however, guiding them toward the norm will prevent another cause of ostracism and bullying.

Some children with NLD are disturbed by patterned clothing. Dr. Rourke tells us that we can attribute deficits in visual perception and in the discrimination and recognition of visual detail to one of the primary neuropsychological deficits that characterizes the syndrome of NLD (Rourke 1989). Although a pattern on fabric may not bother us, we must assume that people with NLD who claim to be uncomfortable with certain designs see the combination of shapes and colors in a way which is disturbing or distracting.

It may be helpful to compare this reaction to a dog that can hear a whistle outside the range of human audiology. We see the dog respond when such a whistle is sounded, but we really don't experience the sonic range to which the animal is responding. Well, some children with NLD have visual reactions outside of the typical sensory range. Although they are responding to things which we cannot see or understand, it is important that we validate their reactions. Obliging them in the desire to wear solid colored clothing is another minor accommodation which will probably not detract from any greatness for which they may be destined. When I have tried to slip in a striped, plaid, or figured shirt with my son's other clothing, it is remarkable only for its pristine condition at the end of the school year. This phenomenon among its ripped, torn, misshapen, and stained associates is due to only one circumstance. It has never been worn.

Some children with NLD get stuck in behavior patterns with clothing that are similar to the rigidities they display in other areas of life, preferring the familiar to exploration and novelty. Often a child with NLD will request a certain brand, color, or style, until you have exhausted the entire quantity of this item the world over. This is the time for parents to engage in creative ways of introducing new styles and brands of clothing. Although I do not have a dispensation from any recognized religious body for this next statement, I believe that parents of children with NLD are free to tell minor prevarications in order to prevent their children from going to school in clothing that is several sizes too small, ripped, held together by one precarious thread in a very compromising location, or stained beyond the boundaries of most Boards of Health.

"Consuela," you might say, "I've learned that your favorite Comfortino Clothing Company has just merged with Jumpin' Jack Jeans. Look, I brought you home a pair of their new soft corduroys, and I've even taken out all the tags so you'll be comfortable. Nothing will itch, scratch, or assault your lower lumbar vertebrae." If you feel more comfortable crossing certain appendages while saying this, or making a donation to charity each time you fabricate such a colossal canard, feel free. The most important thing is to make sure that your child gets used to going out in public fully dressed, even when her favorite pants-maker goes belly up or, in the case of the latest fashion trends, belly out.

Some children will outgrow these acute sensitivities to fabrics and patterns as they mature, others will not. Recently I joined a group of frenzied bargain shoppers in a communal dressing room on a steamy afternoon. One of my favorite boutiques was having a "Welcome to Fall!" sale just when summer decided to have one last hurrah. Nevertheless, I grabbed a few prognosticators of a crisp autumn and joined the optimistic shoppers. Within seconds, I had divested myself of everything but the essentials, and started to pull the lovely striped top of an elegant suit over my head. Suddenly a colony of fire ants in heat invaded every inch of skin from my neck to my waist. I felt as though I were being boiled in itching powder. "Get me out of here!" I screamed. Several of my fellow optimists, probably hoping that they could get a crack at this particular item, were more than happy to take a sleeve and help pull it directly up over my head.

Once revived, I asked one of my rescuers to read the tag. "What is *in* that?" I croaked. "It's 100 per cent virgin wool," she read from the tag. "Virgin," I muttered. That suit had ravaged more women than I would care to count! Just thinking about the fabric made me itch all over. Suddenly I realized that the reaction I had felt was similar to the aversive reaction that kids with NLD feel to fabrics that they can't tolerate. My reaction was less severe, because it was simply topical – I am merely allergic to wool. A reaction sent from the brain, which is what NLDers experience, probably multiplies this feeling a hundredfold.

What do you do, however, when there are occasions which call for specific types of dress? You know that the style or fabric is sure to make your NLDer uncomfortable, but you know that to diverge from the norm may cause certain children the same amount of discomfort. Each family must decide which issues are non-negotiable, and engage help to ensure that their NLDer can be part of the activity on terms which are appropriate for all involved. If you need to begin a program of desensitization to a jacket and tie, do so. Perhaps it is the parents who need to be sensitized to the idea their child can go without a tie. If a dress shirt is stiff and itchy, find a silk one. Can't find one? Have it made. Can't afford to have a silk shirt made? Try polyester. Actually, you'll be a lot happier when you're washing out the inevitable spills.

Do dress shoes feel like pedestrian prisons? Very few people will notice if your child is wearing black sneakers or slip-ons. Just because NLD is an invisible disability doesn't mean it is not a real one. When your child cannot tolerate something, accept that as the truth and find a solution which does not compromise your child's dignity. However, be scrupulous about establishing a bottom line of basic hygiene and never compromise unless you suddenly find yourself cast away on a desert island.

If your child goes away to school, you may find that you have to advocate on his or her behalf to make sure that a potentially positive learning environment isn't poisoned by daily struggles with an uncompromising dress code. Recently, I showed a school to a family which was sure their child could never attend because she categorically refused to wear tights. Her sensorimotor issues and processing speed made it unbearable for her to wrestle with such a complex and annoying piece of clothing every morning. Although the parents were hesitant about requesting alternatives, they learned that many young girls at the school simply wore white sweat pants under their school skirts in the winter and were quite glad of the extra layer in the New England chill. It would be time to renegotiate in spring, but by then we hoped that their daughter would be committed to school and another creative solution could be found.

Similarly, dress codes which require that boys wear ties, collared shirts, or pants with belts often frighten young people with NLD who fear that they will spend half the day getting dressed and the rest of the day feeling uncomfortable in what they have struggled to put on. It is amazing, however, what children can learn when there is positive peer pressure and reinforcement.

I left my son at boarding school when he was 14. No one was allowed into dinner without a jacket and tie, a dress shirt, dress pants, dress socks, and dress shoes with tied laces. All the young gentlemen had to be attired in this formal dinner outfit directly after returning from afternoon sports, and quickly showering. On the way to school, alas only a one-hour ride from home, I frantically tried to teach my son the mechanics of tying a tie quickly. By the time we arrived, I decided that he would either choke himself in the attempt or starve to death because he would never pass inspection for being admitted to dinner. Imagine my surprise when, later that year, he decided to wear a jacket and tie every day to class to feel more like a scholar. The moral – never underestimate the power of an NLDer.

Since some NLDers can be extremely gullible, they often fall victim to the clever advertising campaigns propagated by today's media. One company, for example, promises that its winter gear is undoubtedly the best in the industry and comes with a lifetime guarantee. One NLDer I know rather well decided that this was the only winter jacket to buy. Unfortunately, the price of the jacket was greater than what it would have cost to feed an entire third world country for an average winter. First I tried logic. "You're only 15. Your generation will probably have a life expectancy of 90 years. Why would you want to keep a jacket for so long? Don't you think you'll get bored?" The answer, of course, was "No."

Another tack. "You haven't stopped growing. You need an Extra Large now, which is the biggest size they make. What if you outgrow the jacket in a year or two? What good does it do you if it's guaranteed for life but doesn't fit you?" The frost came. No other jacket was acceptable. I looked in every catalogue, every mall, every outlet. This lifetime experience never went on sale. Why should it? If you amortize the cost over 90 years, it's really a bargain.

Finally, the snows came. He would meet us at the front entrance to school on open weekends in a sweatshirt, his wrists raw with cold and his face beet red. I caved. I bought the jacket. It was warm and soft. He wore it for two winters. Each year he grew a little more until he became six feet and four inches tall. The lifetime jacket began to look as though it was made for a Ken doll. Reluctantly, he agreed that one's bellybutton wasn't supposed to stick out in a snowstorm and we bought a jacket that doesn't come with a lifetime guarantee but that does come in Extra Extra Large. The moral. Never try to outlogic an NLDer.

Many parents of children with NLD have asked me if there is some secret society to which these children belong which involves the ritual cannibalization of clothing. Even the most mild-mannered NLDers are capable of ripping riveted pockets off of pants, slashing shirts to smithereens, and pulling patch pockets off of blazers and coats as if they had been attached with thoughts instead of threads. Shoes which neurotypical children can wear for months seem to undergo an abnormal process of deterioration, going from new to decrepit before the laces are even dirty. One father memorialized his favorite tee-shirt in classic haiku form. Lent to his teenage NLDer, the shirt returned in a reduced state.

My fav'rite T-shirt

Worn by NLD son once

So many holes – how?

(Blim 2003)

As children with NLD grow older, we as parents may see the need for appropriate undergarments long before they do. Although the 1960s made a valiant effort to liberate women from unnecessary underwear, it has never been appropriate for young teenagers to advertise the entire developmental process of secondary sex characteristics in a day-by-day documentary thinly disguised by their tee-shirts. The day will clearly arrive when you see that your daughter needs a bra. If you are a woman, you already know that the quest for a comfortable style can take years. Start with the choice of fabric. By limiting yourself to cotton, you will reduce your possibilities by 90 per cent and make the field much less daunting.

Your daughter will probably prefer that you take her measurements at home. I have not yet met the woman who enjoys being measured in a bra shop. For some reason, the sales clerks are always Amazonian émigrés from some mysterious East European country, with enormous hair and overwhelming perfume. They can make the neurotypical customer feel like an under-ripe cantaloupe in the produce department, so it is wise to shelter your adolescent NLDer from such encounters. If you know her general measurements, you can either bring home a range of samples from a department store and teach her the fine art of buckling and adjusting at home, or you can let her try on possibilities that you have preselected in an undergarment boutique while you guard the door against intruders.

Boys present a different challenge. Occupational therapists can explain that there are two areas on our bodies which contain the most sensory endings. One is the scalp, which usually don't present much of a problem in public, unless it is hosting colonies of creatures not normally expected to reside in that habitat. A boy who scratches his head in public, unless the scratching is related to the aforementioned visitors, is not likely to be considered socially inappropriate. The other repository of multiple sensory endings is the genital area. Most children find out about this sensory subsidy while still in diapers, if not before.

Boys, perhaps because their apparatus is so accessible, often develop the habit of making sure that everything is in the right place and of giving a few manly scratches for a positive sensory experience. As they mature, however, there are complications attached to genital sensory pleasure, and some adolescents find it rather important to check on the equipment with little regard for appropriateness of time or place. If your son has been wearing boxer shorts because they offer minimal contact with his body and minimal possibility of sensory discomfort, you might want to suggest that he is no longer anatomically suited for free-form and accessible underwear.

Because children with sensory integration problems get sensory messages differently from their peers, your son may have more difficulty deflecting the messages his body is sending him. Many adolescent boys with NLD feel less overwhelmed by these sensory broadcasts and are better able to concentrate on other work when they switch to snug jockey shorts. For some, it might even be necessary to suggest that they wear tight bicycle shorts over their underwear and under their outer trousers in order to keep their sensory distractions quiescent until their private moments.

Another challenge for the parents of adolescent NLDers is helping them learn to shop for clothing themselves, another lesson on the path toward becoming productive, independent adults. This experience may make them lifelong devotees of mail order catalogues, but that, too, is an independent decision. Be prepared to consider their neuropsychological assets and deficits when you go shopping with your NLDers. Most people with NLD are overwhelmed by large department stores with multiple options, scores of overly stimulating displays, and offensive fragrancemongers hawking the latest designer perfume. They are more comfortable in small stores that cater to simple practical styles where they can find what they need, try it on (albeit under duress), and get home. In fact, some parents of younger children with NLD prefer to buy clothing second-hand because it has already been washed enough to be soft and pliable. Gargantuan department stores were made for people who love to shop and enjoy the opportunity to outfit an entire household and its inhabitants in a single outing. NLDers can actually experience physical discomfort in such settings.

Finally, for every child with NLD who fits the characteristics above, there is one who loves to shop, enjoys all types of clothing, and defies every description attributed to the typical patterns of NLDers and clothing. That is the blessing and the curse of the syndrome of NLD. It is recreated anew in each person who carries the diagnosis and it is up to parents and caregivers to be sensitive to each child's specific requirements. It is also our responsibility to guarantee that our children retain the possibility of being accepted by the mainstream. While quirky, eccentric children can be charming and wonderful, wearing a silky Superman cape to sixth grade can cause serious social setbacks. Although it's always inappropriate to force, we must use logical and gentle ways to explain the range of appropriate dress and the reasons for certain sartorial conventions.

Since Eve ate the apple, it has been imperative in most societies to get dressed every day. This makes the struggle with clothing ongoing and incessant. If you find yourself losing the battle against your NLDer's tactile defensiveness and sensory dysfunction and are not in a position to relocate to a nudist colony, enlist the help of a qualified professional. Remember, the parents of NLDers are not required to wear superhero capes, even though they often seem called upon to perform superhero acts of parenting.

A good occupational therapist should be able to develop a desensitization program for your child which might expand the range of clothing types that feel more comfortable. When your child is at an age to appreciate it, treat your child to this NLD-appropriate witticism by American humorist Mark Twain:

> Clothes make the man. Naked people have little or no influence in society.
>
> *(Twain 1997, p.54)*

Key points

1. Parents of children and teenagers with NLD must help them learn to dress in a way which will keep them comfortable enough to focus on other life tasks while looking acceptable enough to fit into the mainstream and to avoid ridicule.

2. Make sure that you help your NLDers comply with their needs in an understanding way. Never make fun of a clothing preference dictated by neurological need. Compliment your children when they are neatly dressed (try to catch them early

in the day!) and help them feel attractive and appropriately dressed.

3. If you find yourself losing the battle against your NLDer's tactile defensiveness and sensory dysfunction and are not in a position to relocate to a nudist colony, find a good occupational therapist.

4. NLDers may not realize that clothing needs change as their bodies develop during adolescence. Keep an open dialogue so that you can help with awareness of appropriate clothing styles and behaviors.

5. Even when certain occasions require specific styles of dress, try to make your NLDer as comfortable as possible. It is better to break an unwritten dress code than to cause stress or a meltdown.

Chapter Nine

Holidays

The most important guarantors of equanimity in the lives of children with NLD are safety and consistency. The most characteristic features of holiday celebrations are surprise and change. You don't need an advanced degree in logic to realize that everything that makes holidays exciting for neurotypical children and adults makes people with NLD retreat into the darkest recesses of the cranial labyrinth. Special holiday foods, wonderful once-a-year smells, guests we see rarely, decorations which replace everyday household objects energize the neurotypicals while they enervate our loved ones with NLD. Does this mean that NLDers have no holiday spirit? Of course not! Does this mean that we have to observe every holiday with the celebration meter on low and the menu set to bland? Not unless those are particular religious customs you enjoy. If you want your NLDers to enjoy the essence of any holiday, all you have to do is think, consider, and plan. In addition, it would probably be a good idea to cut down on firecrackers and unexpected visitors like young ladies who pop out of fruit cakes.

Interestingly, when you design your holidays and special occasions with the NLDer in mind, you will find that every sort of guest you could imagine entertaining will reap the benefits of your thoughtful planning. Until your NLDer is out of the house and living a happy independent life, it might be a good idea to consider putting spontaneity on hold. In order to get through the holiday with your spirit (and your spirits!) intact, you'll need to make careful plans concerning menus, transitions, noise level at any parties you are planning, people you would like to invite to celebrations at home, events you expect to attend with your NLDer, and travel plans if your family intends to vacation together anywhere beyond the back yard.

Rick Lavoie (2002), a nationally recognized speaker, writer, and authority on learning disabilities, often reminds parents to "Prepare the child for the situation, and prepare the situation for the child." For families with NLD, this is a far more appropriate holiday toast than "Cheers!" Remember that children with NLD process the world auditorily. For them, your word is a verbal contract. When you say, "We are going to visit Uncle Obadiah," you *are* going to visit Uncle Obadiah. The details are secondary. So, in order to make sure that you don't set your children up for a series of disappointments, involve them in the planning, and make sure they understand that everything is only a possibility until all details are final.

"Let's think of some places to consider visiting during school vacation. We might take a few days to visit Uncle Obadiah. Would you like to see how the farm looks in winter? Remember, this is just a possibility, but I can promise you that I'll look into it." When you bring up ideas in this way, you are saving your child from disappointment and yourself from a barrage of bitter recriminations. Then, of course, you have to see if comfortable travel arrangements can be made (three-stop plane trips or five-hour car rides are never a great choice), if Uncle Obadiah is feeling well and has enough help to incorporate the incursion of five souls into his bachelor household, and if the weather will cooperate with the skiing and sleigh rides you might have carelessly mentioned in a moment of wishful weakness.

If you do choose to visit relatives, it will be important to discuss your child with your relatives, and, more important, to discuss your relatives with your child. Tell Aunt Sarah, the cheek chucker, that Jonas might be traumatized for life if she runs after him, swoops him up in her prodigious arms, and pinches a monumental expanse of cheek between her thumb and forefinger while crowing, "Oy, such a doll! A face like this you see only on an angel!"

Just in case Sarah doesn't get it, and gets Jonas instead, explain to him in advance that this is a gesture of love and not a call to arms. You can even spend some time looking through family albums before you leave, remind-ing him, "Look Jonas, here's Aunt Sarah, the cheek chucker. She makes the best chocolate chip cookies you'll ever taste and she's the sweetest of Grandpa's sisters, but she just can't resist chucking a cherubic cheek!"

If you are planning a party for adults, ask your child if there is someone he or she would like to invite for an evening of pizza and videos. If, as is too often the case for children with NLD, such a friend is hard to find, see if you can locate a charismatic caregiver, perhaps a college student or older cousin, who will plan an evening of alternate activities so that your child does not feel left out. Some children with NLD are very comfortable with adults. If you believe that your child will fit in with your friends, assign an age-appro-priate task, such as greeter, coat-taker, or even official bearer of the *hors d'oeuvres* tray (a light and unbreakable tray, of course), so that he or she can socialize for a short time before leaving your group. This can be a great opportunity for building self-esteem and practicing social skills.

If you are planning a party for children, make sure that this is an event your child truly wants, and not something that you have decided is appro-priate. Many years ago, before I understood the ramifications of NLD, I planned a raucous party for my child at a pizza and game party palace where anthropomorphized mechanical animals played discordant music and sang infantile songs at decibels designed to destroy even the most neurotypical eardrums.

Most of his classmates roared with delight every time the chaotic clatter began. But I will never forget the look on my son's face as he stared at me like a deer caught in the headlights, totally paralyzed by sensory overload. Wanting to make him beloved, admired, and envied by his classmates, I had planned a party that nine out of ten kids would adore. Unfortunately, he was the tenth.

Many holidays center around events which require children and adults to dress more elegantly than they usually do for school, work, or even year-round social occasions. Some adults enjoy the trappings of finery, and there are even some children who adore getting all dressed up, as long as it isn't too frequent an occurrence. For children with NLD, however, most dress clothes are even more uncomfortable than their everyday clothes. Make sure to have a trial run in any outfits you expect them to wear to reli-gious services or to fancy social events. There are adaptations you can make in advance which will make the event much less stressful. By removing tags, lining itchy parts with smooth fabric, and adjusting places that pinch, pull, or simply annoy, you are doing everything possible to prevent a clothing catastrophe.

Unless you live in a Winnebago, chances are that you will be away from your kitchen and your child's favorite foods when you are traveling. Children with NLD have a tendency to be particularly sensitive to tastes, smells, and textures, and are known for eating a very limited diet. They tend to rely on a fairly restricted number of unadventurous staples for comfort and nutrition, although some become inexplicably attached to foods that are especially sour, crunchy, salty, or otherwise extreme. If your child is particularly attached to a specific food, make sure that you bring plenty of it with you wherever you go. Don't look at vacation time as an opportunity to break Horatio of his addiction to pickled watermelon rind. You will soon be redefining the term "vacation."

All of us have connections to certain foods that give us sensory pleasure, much like Proust's *madeleine*. Children who suffer from disorders of sensory integration, like many NLDers, can develop an acuity of sensory aversion or attraction that is remarkably profound. However, we can begin to understand some of their reactions when we examine our own behavior. My husband, who now lives thousands of miles from the Australian continent, spent the first nine years of his life in Melbourne. I had never considered the Australians a nation of child abusers until I tasted the noxious brown paste called Vegemite that they feed their children. What's worse, they seem to have brainwashed an entire nation of children into thinking that this glutinous spread, ostensibly a combination of road tar and salt, is a tasty and healthy alternative to normal childhood fare like peanut butter. My husband, who has otherwise coped with five decades of life in fairly reasonable ways, is addicted to this odious adulteration. At times, I have been reduced to ordering it from Australia just so that he could ruin a perfectly good piece of toast with a smear of childhood.

Those of you who will travel miles for a Mallomar, *you know who you are.* Think what happens when you *must* have one. And even then, reduced by a relentless craving to venture out in a nightgown and trenchcoat to the all night convenience store, you are still more in charge of your sensory responses than your NLDer. You are also an adult. Therefore, it is unequivocally your responsibility to make sure that your child has comfort food available at all times, even if these foods seem oddly uncomforting to you. This dictum should be enforced even more strongly during times that may increase anxiety, like holidays, travel, and transition. These are also optimal times, by the way, to stay on good terms with a qualified pediatric dentist.

If you are considering bringing your family to a destination which has a vacation camp for children, make sure to speak with experienced camp officials and not just your travel agent before you dream of depositing your little ones in another's care while you and your mate chatter childlessly in the sun and surf. Children with NLD do not react well to superimposed transitions and rigidly enforced schedules that they do not understand. Activities which are above or beneath their academic, sensorimotor, or visuospatial skill levels can send them into severe and immediate reactions of meltdown or shutdown. This, in turn, will ensure that they are deposited forthwith at the closed flap of your love cabana, no matter what activities were planned or in progress. Before you travel, you should understand which situations trigger your child's worst behavior and why. Then it is up to you to make sure that these triggers do not recur routinely at your destination.

Children with NLD need a place to decompensate and refuel from even the most carefully designed vacation plans. Whether you are staying home, taking day trips, traveling to an exotic destination, visiting relatives, or hiding out in a remote getaway, make sure that there is a special place where your NLDer can be comfortably alone, away from the crowd, and engaged in a relaxing and appropriate activity. Explain that everyone gets overwhelmed sometimes, and that people who want to stay emotionally healthy should learn to cope with stress and overload from the time they are very young. Actually, we'd all be much happier if we took time out every afternoon to stretch out with a juice box and a blankie just when the stress of the day begins to build. Unfortunately, this is frowned upon in the adult world unless you are in a spa where you can pay enormous sums of money for the very same privilege.

Kids with NLD have difficulty finding words to deflect their anxieties and need to find ways to help expel the tension from their bodies. By identifying spots where they can feel safe to relax, think things over, and get some proprioceptive feedback, you can help them help the entire family enjoy vacation time. Although many parents try to prevent children from watching television or playing video games, these can actually be relaxing activities for children with NLD, because the consistency and mindlessness of these activities displaces some external tension that may have accumulated from events of the day. All TV and video involvement, of course, should be monitored for time and content. There can definitely be too much of a good thing. You should also check before you leave home to see if your child would prefer to bring books on tape, CDs, or favorite movies, and make sure that there will be the correct equipment to activate them.

The holiday dinner, whatever holiday it marks, is not the time to expect your NLDer to make a culinary breakthrough. Personally, I have never really known what is the basis for sticky pudding or what could possibly be in a Yule Log that would make anyone want to eat something by that name. I imagine that guests in my home might get a bit confused or even fearful when I say I am going into the kitchen to bring out the *tzimmes* or the *kugel*, staples of my New Year feast. So if your NLDer prefers to have a small bowl of pasta with a dollop of margarine (the NLD gourmet standard) while you are serving *foie gras flambé*, make sure that you have a smile and a serving ready in the kitchen.

During the holidays, whether you stay home or venture out, there can be noise levels and sensory stimuli that differ from the sounds of the school year. Singers on street corners, aggressive vendors both on the street and inside stores, and ebullient people sharing holiday wishes in all varieties of personal discipline can make even neurotypicals wish that they had a volume control for real-world noise. Some children with NLD may not be bothered by the sounds of holiday cheer, some may be mildly disconcerted, and others may lose all ability to handle themselves effectively during such an assault on their sensory systems. Watch your child carefully for responses to noises, decorations, and other stimuli that may be frightening and overwhelming. Preview things that you know might happen, and explain others that happen suddenly. When you see that your NLDer is becoming defensive and disorganized, change all plans and find a comfort zone before the frustration level turns into a meltdown.

Some holidays bring the added challenge of customary gift-giving. For NLDers, who often have great trouble understanding the perspective of others, giving and receiving gifts can be a difficult social responsibility. If it is the custom in your family to have everyone give gifts, help your NLDer understand how to think of a gift that will make its recipient feel happy and appreciated. Help children understand why gifts are given, what we want the person receiving our gift to think and feel, and what we can do to elicit those thoughts and feelings.

As difficult as it is to give a gift, it can be even harder to teach a child to accept a gift graciously. Since NLDers are known for their forthright and openly expressed opinions, it is helpful to role play situations for accepting gifts graciously. "My Mom told me she would never let me play with anything like that" is not the best thing to tell Cousin Gardenia, who cares for retired racing greyhounds and rarely approaches human beings under 40 years old. It's never a good idea to suggest telling lies, but NLDers love rules. If you make it clear that the rule is to accept a gift by saying "thank you," chances are no one will think your child has been raised by demons.

If you are buying a gift for a person with NLD, remember to take that person's unique characteristics into consideration when choosing something special. Factor learning style, sensory issues, social preferences, and motor abilities into the decision. Don't buy a gift that represents a physical challenge you want a child to live up to or a fear you hope she will overcome. A gift should make the recipient feel, "Someone really knows me and cares about me just the way I am."

Since the holiday season can disrupt even the most systematic minds, it's always a good idea to continually reinforce the lessons directed at enjoying the season and at dispelling disasters of mood, deed, and disposition. The good news is that most holidays come to an end more quickly than most celebrants would like. However, in the case of families with NLD, there may also be problems as children transition back into the routine world of school and the daily schedule. Expect some difficulty with the transition, and store an extra helping of patience for the fluctuations that accompany post-vacation re-entry.

Even if you follow all the rules, pre-test all the conditions, and prescreen all the destinations, there will always be one holiday component whose reactions you can never anticipate with total accuracy – your child. Many NLDers, despite their true desire to take pleasure in a holiday or vacation, cannot feel free enough to relinquish the conditions that restrict them to rigid definitions of good and bad. As soon as one thing happens which falls outside of their expectations, they tend to default to gloom and despair. In

Chapter 14, we will discuss the range of possibilities between all black or all white. Once NLDers learn that an experience can be fun even if one or two components aren't perfect, they can learn to enjoy many more of life's little pleasures.

You can simplify the lives of children with NLD and guarantee both these children and the rest of your family a happier and more peaceful holiday season if you preserve the two elements that help NLDers function at their best – *safety* and *consistency*. As long as you make it clear that you have taken care of their physical and emotional needs, and follow through on that promise with consistency and continued credibility, children with NLD will gradually rely on your word and begin to reduce the extreme anxiety and inflexibility which holds them hostage. By relaxing, they minimize their tendency toward meltdowns, and make themselves more available to satisfying social interactions.

A Safe and Consistent Holiday Season to all NLDers, and to all a Good Night!

Key points

1. Everything that makes holidays exciting for neurotypical children and adults is confusing and unsettling for people with NLD, who are uncomfortable with unexpected events and change in routine.

2. If you want your NLDers to enjoy the essence of any holiday, all you have to do is think, consider, and plan.

3. Children with NLD need a place to decompensate and refuel from even the most carefully designed vacation plans. Whether you are staying home, taking day trips, traveling to an exotic destination, visiting relatives, or hiding out in a remote getaway, make sure that there is a special place where your NLDer can be comfortably alone, away from the crowd, and engaged in a relaxing and appropriate activity.

4. Kids with NLD have difficulty finding words to deflect their
    anxieties and need to find ways to help expel the tension from
    their bodies. By identifying spots where they can feel safe to
    relax, think things over, and get some proprioceptive feedback,
    you can help them help the entire family enjoy holidays and
    vacations.

Chapter Ten

Hurrying

There is really only one thing to know about hurrying when dealing with people who have NLD: They can't. In fact, if I didn't feel inclined to give some explanation and cite some examples, I would end this chapter here. However, I believe that it is important to help family members modify their behaviors and expectations so that they can deal effectively with people who are neurologically unable to change theirs.

When neurotypical people realize that there is a possibility of arriving late for something that is scheduled for a specific time, they do a quick mental prioritization of the following facts related to the meeting or appointment:

- Does it matter if I am late?

- What will be the effect of my lateness?

- Will I lose anything important by arriving late?

- How will my lateness affect my relationship with the people I am supposed to see?

- Is there anything I can do to reverse the possibility of lateness?

Most people don't even deliberately make lists to establish these priorities; the whole scenario springs full-blown into consciousness like Athena from Zeus's head. Then, still on automatic pilot, the priorities sift themselves into subsets of response or denial with possibilities and consequences.

Does it matter if I am late?
Of course. This hairdresser insists that you arrive promptly.

Will I lose anything by being late?
I'll probably never get another appointment if I'm not careful about arriving on time.

How will my lateness affect my relationship with the people I am supposed to see?
Mr. Alonzo will be snippy and will probably snip me within an inch of my skull.

Is there anything I can do to reverse the possibility of lateness?

- I could skip breakfast and let my stomach gurgle throughout the haircut.
- I could speed, but if I got stopped, I'd arrive even later.
- I could call ahead to say I'm running late, but then he'd assume for sure that I didn't "value" his time.
- I could put all my activities from now to then on double time, take the back road to avoid lights, *and* skip breakfast. That should save me about ten minutes, and if he's talking with a customer and I rush to put on the salon robe as soon as I arrive, he may not even notice that I arrived a few minutes late.

Or, in another case:

Does it matter if I am late?
Not really. Every time I go to the dentist, I have to wait at least fifteen minutes to be seen, so I probably have a few minutes to work with after the specific time for which the appointment is scheduled.

Will I lose anything by being late?

Of course. I want to show the staff the courtesy they show me so that I can have their cooperation when I have a problem or emergency.

How will my lateness affect my relationship with the people I am supposed to see?

I don't want Dr. Frankenstein to think that I am belittling his professionalism.

Is there anything I can do to reverse the possibility of lateness?

Yes, I can cancel the errand I was planning to do on the way. I can reschedule the client I am expecting right before I have to leave for the dentist so there is no possibility of running over. I can take a cab so I won't have to circle for 20 minutes looking for a parking spot.

For most people, all of the processing which leads to a decision regarding the most efficient way to either arrive on time or minimize the degree of lateness takes place in a manner that seems almost simultaneous. Into one slot goes the question "How can I avoid being late?" and out of another pop the viable alternatives or lack thereof. The neurotypical system adjusts and proceeds with Plan B. For people with NLD, however, processing for an unexpected eventuality or a random change in schedule is protracted and arduous.

What processes can hurrying affect?

Visual/spatial/organizational

The need to hurry affects all of the systems which are inherently the most difficult for people with NLD to handle – the visual-spatial/organizational, the sensorimotor, and the social. Hurrying, especially when imposed on them by an external source, is a multisystem assault that at best causes disorientation and at worst can engender completely dysfunctional behavior. We know that children and adults with NLD are most comfortable when they have adjusted to a pattern of behavior by practicing it in the same way over an extended period of time. Expecting them to change spontaneously because they woke up late, because of a problem on the highway, or because of another serendipitous circumstance, is rather like training a skunk not to spray. You might eventually succeed, but compared to the disadvantages, the benefits would stink.

I once tried to explain the comfort and necessity of morning ritual to the mother of an NLDer who was in my office with her son. "NLDers," I explained patiently, "have a difficult time making the transition from sleep to wakefulness. It is very important to let them go through whatever paces in the morning make them feel ready to face the day." I told them both that this transition should always be age appropriate and that if school or a job required that the NLDer be present at specific hours, the family could definitely intervene at first to help generate a response to an appropriate time-line. Once established, however, I explained to the mother, the schedule would be more or less inflexible and that it would take a situation of major impact to encourage the NLDer to change the pace or priority of morning activity. Trying to make a point, I said, "Why, even if I told a person with NLD that there was a fire in the house, I'm sure that he or she would shower, dress, go down to the kitchen for breakfast, and move a bit more quickly only if the actual flames were making it somewhat uncomfortable to sit at the kitchen table and read the newspaper."

The mother looked at her son as though I had just told her he was the spawn of mutant bacteria from the planet Pluto. "That's what you would do if the house was on fire?" she asked him.

"Well, yeah," he admitted. "I probably would do whatever it was that I had to do first. But if it were really a big fire and I could see that it was a matter of life and death I would run outside. I'm not an idiot. But one thing I could tell you for sure. I would feel very disoriented if I couldn't do the things I usually do in the morning."

Radiating astonishment, the mother asked, "It wouldn't disorient you if the house were burning down?"

"Well, ultimately, sure," her son answered ingenuously, "but first I would have to get over being all weirded out from the messed up morning."

Often, when a neurotypical parent is stressed by an impending appointment or by the fact that she feels like a hare who has given birth to a tortoise, she may decide that raising her voice is a logical way to compensate for her child's poky processing. After all, the fact that her child did not respond to her first fifteen "encouragements" must mean that he didn't hear her urging him to hurry.

"MERRRRRRRRRR-LINNNNNNNNNNNNNNN!
MOOOOOOOOOOOVE IT!" she suggests demurely, assuming that this
time he is certain to hear. But, in fact, children with sensory problems may,
in fact, be less likely to hear tones which they find intolerable. In *The Out-of-Sync Child*, Carol Kranowitz tells us that children with supersensitive
auditory systems can become so uncomfortable when they hear
high-pitched or loud voice tones that they may totally misinterpret what is
said or even become totally overwhelmed and distraught. She relates from
her own experience:

> One day I had to use a more forceful voice than usual to move a
> group... I didn't understand then...why a particularly anxious boy
> cried, "Don't talk to me that way! Don't you know I can't do
> anything right when you talk to me that way?"
>
> *(Kranowitz 1998, pp.231–2)*

Another organizational issue which many of us take for granted – time – is a
topic which will always remain mysterious to many people with NLD. They
never seem to develop a true awareness of elapsed time, and for this reason,
many are unable to judge how much time is necessary to complete a certain
function. Without specifically clocking the time spent, they would probably
be unable to estimate how long it takes to complete even routine functions
that they perform daily, such as getting dressed, showering, or shaving. If
you wait until the last moment to tell them that a class schedule or appointment time has changed, they may be unable to spontaneously make a corre-
sponding change in their routines.

Neurotypical teenagers, on learning that school opening will be delayed
an hour due to a snowstorm, will automatically reset the alarm and go
through their exact routine one hour later and in a considerably happier
mood. Many NLDers I know, however, seem to believe that this delay
should enable them to sleep until ten minutes before the bus is due, despite
the fact that they usually take much longer than ten minutes to get ready for
school in the morning. This has nothing to do with math difficulties, since
there are many NLDers who are atypically gifted in higher math concepts.
To explain this in the most scientifically detailed terms, these miscalcula-
tions are simply due to a characteristically quirky relationship with time.

Sensory/motor

Clearly, having to change an organizational process which is working well will generate problems for most NLDers. Asking them to hurry also puts demands on sensory motor functions which can render tasks that they have learned to do effortlessly almost impossible. For most people with typical motor skills, getting dressed is not a particularly rigorous activity. Though it can be difficult choosing what to wear or adapting to the latest styles, the actual physical act of putting clothes on our bodies, buttoning them, snapping them, or zipping them, is not an overwhelming challenge.

Some NLDers, however, have fingers which don't receive signals for coordinated activity from their brains. For them, achieving dexterity is like running an obstacle course blindfolded. The fact that most NLDers learn to perform these activities despite the mixed signals is an incredible accomplishment. They draw on resources of perseverance, determination, patience, and plain old obstinacy until they master these activities of daily living. But when you yell upstairs, "Hurry, Pernicia, we have an appointment with the otolaryngologist and we'll be late if we don't leave in 32 seconds," all the well-trained fingers turn into thumbs. And there's very little you can do with a set of ten thumbs (even well-trained ones), unless you aspire to become a member of the Olympic Thumb Wrestling Team.

Social

The social aspect of a situation can also suffer if a person with NLD is forced to hurry when he or she hasn't factored in haste beforehand. Many NLDers like to prepare themselves for meetings, appointments, or other interpersonal encounters by previewing and rehearsing the scene verbally, reminding themselves of their relationships with the people involved, or by trying to recall, in whatever modality serves them best, the people, places, and things involved. Some even like to prepare a few phrases to use, a story to tell, or a joke to share. When this process is interrupted and they are forced to enter a situation prematurely, they can experience extreme discomfort.

Helping a child with NLD maintain functionality in the face of unanticipated change is one of the non-negotiable tasks of parenting these challenging and rewarding children. If you don't help them understand that normal lives have peaks and valleys, you will not have prepared your children to live independently. Although most families devise coping strategies that are best suited to the unique temperaments of each NLDer and, by extension, each family, some of the suggestions below can be adapted for global use.

The white lie accommodation

I believe that embellishing the truth in extenuating circumstances for a person's good is a redeemable wrongdoing, a mere misdemeanor on the spectrum of sin. Of course, when our NLDers do it to us, it is called unconscionable manipulation, but when we do it for the good of our NLDers, it is called the little white lie. Since I am a woman of impeccable ethical character (Halo Size – Ethereal #1), I employ this accommodation only in relation to procrastination, preparedness, and appointment times. Whenever I had to take my young NLDer to an appointment, I always changed the time by half an hour. If I had scheduled an appointment at 4:30, I told him that it was scheduled for 4:00. That allowed him to start getting ready in a time frame that he thought would enable us to arrive at 4:00, though I always knew that we would squeak into the parking lot at about 4:29. Yes, *mea culpa*, I lied. Frequently. But what I was doing was really a kindness.

Look at it this way. Instead of reminding a child every time he had an appointment that he has a neurological disability which makes it impossible for him to allot the appropriate amount of time to tasks requiring organization, I simply said, "Your appointment's at 4:00." I never deluded myself about the fact that I was lying, but I always believed that the ends justified the means. In fact, I was so convinced of my righteousness that I rationalized my prevarication using the philosophy of a renowned Harvard professor of moral development.

The late Lawrence Kohlberg developed the Heinz Dilemma to gauge whether people were justice-oriented or relationship-oriented in their interpretation of morality. Kohlberg asked people to decide whether a poor man should be considered innocent or guilty for stealing medicine he could not afford to buy to save his dying wife. Those who maintained that the sanctity of human life far outweighs any system of law and therefore nullifies the magnitude of the theft were considered relationship-oriented. Those who rigidly insisted that theft was theft and that the law could not be adjusted for individual circumstance were coded as justice-oriented. Ironically, most

NLDers would probably choose the justice orientation. Luckily, they have parents who will often simplify a situation by sanctifying relationship. By the power granted in me as the mother of one and educator of many NLDers, I hereby absolve all of us who love them of the little white lies we tell on their behalf.

The Book on Tape Remediation

The Book on Tape Remediation methodology has been especially designed as a multimodal system for diverting the natural inclination of Type A parents and caregivers to jumpstart the natural NLD inclination toward Type Z personality. Most of us are familiar with the characteristics of Type A – the frenetic personality type known for multitasking at a hectic pace. Type Z, though rarely invoked in the taxonomy of common personality types, is the natural default of most people diagnosed with NLD. Type Zs are deliberate and dawdling in the fulfillment of their daily duties. Though they may have voluminous vocabularies, the word "hurry" is rarely within them. Even if they were neurologically able to do two things at once, they would consider doing so an illogical pursuit. The Type Z is the natural irritant of the Type A. If the two types are forced to share preparation for the same task in the same space, it is wise to alert the local paramedics well in advance. The Type A will probably suffer cardiac arrest from frustration while the Type Z goes into shock from disbelief.

This is where The Book on Tape Remediation system is invaluable for both parties. Instead of remaining in the house and yelling "Hurry up, we're late!" at regular intervals in increasing decibels, the Type A completes his or her preparation and retreats to the family car with a Book on Tape. The best of all tapes is some riveting tale which completely distracts the Type A from the fact that time is rushing by and the Type Z is not. The Type A should then remove all sensory connection with the Type Z by closing the car windows, turning on the air conditioning (or heat where required), and starting to play the Book on Tape. If snacks help, this remediation can be catered, according to individual dietary preference. In most cases, full engagement with alternative reality will help the Type A pass time peacefully and productively until the Type Z NLDer is ready to join you for your mutual engagement.

Accept as a given that your Type Z children cannot redirect their energies or change the pace of their lives. But you can take control of yours while you still have the ability to do so. Instead of letting "NLD moments" drive you crazy bemoaning things you can never change, use these unexpected bonuses to recharge for the challenges to come. You'll be amazed at how quickly you can get through *War and Peace*. You can even keep a Hershey's kiss in the glove compartment for those days when you really need a snuggle.

Preparing for independence

As your NLDers mature, you can start helping them develop systems which will make it easier to get to school, work, or appointments on time. As soon as they can read, you can make a list to hang in the bathroom of morning hygiene rituals. Since NLDers respond gratefully to rules, you will find that these non-negotiable morning activity lists can save your NLDer many trips to brush teeth or hair that have acquired accumulations of unidentifiable attributes overnight. As they grow older, you can teach them to listen to weather reports and prepare clothing at night. You can even teach your children to check weather pages on the Internet to see if they will need raincoats or boots in the morning. Many NLDers are natural superstars at gathering information.

Developing the habit of organizing school things in the evening can prevent the intolerable morning marathon of running all over the house to find inanimate objects that must surely have come alive while everyone was sleeping and have inexplicably hidden in the house's darkest nooks and crannies. There's not a parent in the world who wouldn't trade the bedlam of the post-breakfast scavenger hunt for some planned post-dinner packing.

You can also teach your NLDers to accept unexpected eventualities by consistently using language that anticipates the possibility of change. "We have an appointment with the dentist right after school today, as long as Dr. Frankenstein doesn't have any unexpected emergency patients in his office this afternoon." If your NLDer has already heard of the possibility that schedules can change, he or she will not become totally disoriented if possibility turns into reality. NLDers are predisposed to accept routine. It is our responsibility to help them weather change and transition by introducing it gently and gradually into their lives. This will also guarantee a quicker and more coordinated response to any new agenda since they will not have to regroup completely to reorient themselves to the change in plans.

Finally, not all family members respond in the same way to any given set of circumstances. Responses vary with or without regard to classifications of NLD or neurotypical. Think how a family like your own might react if suddenly informed that you had won a two-week vacation to an exotic locale. Within half an hour, my second son and I would be packed, ready to go, and looking out the window for the airport taxi. Of course, his bag would contain one tee-shirt and a pair of shorts and mine would require the ministrations of an Olympic weight-lifter, but we would nevertheless be at the door and waiting for the cab in no time at all.

Son number one would be on the phone informing everyone he knew of his good fortune and finding out every cool thing to do at our destination. He would commandeer his youngest brother to pack for him according to specific instructions and then notice that the same youngest brother, the NLDer, was totally clueless as to what was happening. He would complain a bit, ask his mother what the youngest brother needed, and then pack him a bag generously but a bit pedantically. My daughter would spend a great deal of time worrying about the safety of our destination, then spend an equal amount of time worrying about what to pack. Ultimately, she too would join us at the door in a triumph of self-sufficiency and trust. My husband would check the validity of the offer, examine the passports, call the bank, organize for our transportation to and from the airport, handle all the arrangements for our safe arrival and departure, and appear impeccably dressed and packed just as the taxi pulled up to the door.

What is important to understand from this anecdote is that everyone dealt with the situation in a different way, but everyone made it to the door on time and ready to go. Be sure to understand which way your NLDer does things. Be sure you know which family member makes him or her feel safest when there are sudden changes in plans. Know the chain of command and know the chain of support. Praise all members of your family for a job well done.

In today's hectic world, perhaps it is our NLDers who can teach us something about hurrying. Don't force them to alter their tempo unless disaster or distress looms. Alter your pace to match theirs. You may end up enjoying the benefits of the gift you give your children.

Now, here, you see, it takes all the running you can do, to keep in the same place. If you want to get somewhere else, you must run at least twice as fast as that!

(Carroll 2002)

Key points

1. The need to hurry affects all of the systems which are inherently the most difficult for people with NLD to handle – the visual-spatial/organizational, the sensorimotor, and the social. Hurrying, especially when imposed externally, is a multisystem assault that at best causes disorientation and at worst can engender completely dysfunctional behavior.

2. Helping to maintain functionality in the face of unanticipated change is one of the non-negotiable tasks of parenting NLDers. If you don't help them understand that normal lives have peaks and valleys, you will not have prepared your children to live independently.

3. Make sure to understand which way your NLDer operates. Be sure you know which family member makes him or her feel safest when there are sudden changes in plans.

4. NLDers have difficulty developing a true perception of elapsed time. This makes it puzzling for them to figure out how much time is necessary to complete a certain function. Help them become aware of how long it takes to perform certain routine activities so that they can learn to plan ahead.

5. NLDers are not capable of altering the neurobiological signals which regulate the pace of their activities. As the neurotypicals in their lives, we must engender the compromise between education and accommodation. We have more flexibility to alter our behaviors and expectations.

Chapter Eleven

Illness

Late one afternoon, after allowing the recuperative after-school alone time, the mother of a nine-year-old with NLD walked upstairs to his room to see if there was anything he might like. Upon entering, she was astonished to see that his left arm was heavily wrapped in silver duct tape from wrist to elbow. Silently, she berated herself. "How could I have missed that when he came in? Is he hurt, was he being bullied, is he Robbie the Robot in a school play?" There was nothing her son hated more than a shrill voice or what he called "being infantilized." Gathering a preternatural calm, she spoke: "Hon, what's going on there with your arm?"

"I got scratched at school," he replied, with a slight quaver in his voice.

"Scratched?" she asked herself. "By what, a saber-tooth tiger? A great white shark? The Loch Ness monster?" Calming down, she queried kindly, "Didn't we have any band-aids?"

"It's too big for what we have," he answered bravely.

"I think I'll have to see it," she said resolutely, wincing internally at the ordeal that she knew awaited them both. "Duct tape isn't too good for scratches, because it has adhesive on the inside. When you pull it off, it will make everything worse. The sooner you remove it, the better."

The dialogue that ensued is not worth recording. But ultimately the two arrived at the moment of revelation. The son, moaning and teary, faced the wall as his mother unwound layer after layer of heavy tape from the mercifully hairless forearm. The final stratum was about to be removed. Mom felt like Howard Carter at King Tut's tomb. Suddenly an expanse of bare arm was revealed and when the debris cleared, there lay the scratch – a pale superficial wound less than a millimeter long, which looked as though it had been inflicted by a passing twig or at best the errant corner of a paperback book.

Parents, beware. This is no laughing matter. To your NLDer, this is as serious as the severed artery he believes it to be. Treating it with any less dignity would be negating your child's true fears and emotions. Treat first, teach later.

"Oh dear," said the mother gravely, "we need to take care of this right away." She retreated to the bathroom, allegedly to get first aid supplies out of the medicine cabinet. While she was there, however, she used the opportunity to run the water at its highest and flush the toilet noisily to chuckle a bit at the voluminous duct tape "cast" and the tiny red scratch. Mothers of NLDers should take every opportunity to laugh, even if you have to flush the toilet noisily to drown yourself out. It may affect your plumbing somewhat, but it's always preferable to crying. Sometimes our children are distressingly disempowered by their fears. As parents, we need to stay astonishingly upbeat to pull them to the other side.

Mom then returned somberly to her son's room and proceeded to dress the "wound." Obviously, she and any other person of minimal intelligence could have seen that this scratch was so minor it hardly qualified for a band-aid. Yet the son was completely serious about his assessment of the injury and concern for its consequences. Was he a hemophiliac descendant of the Russian nobility? Hardly. He has NLD. His arm had been unblemished and now the skin was broken. It had bled. He was injured. For many people who have NLD, things are either all good or all bad. His arm had been all good. In fact, he hadn't given it a thought until he got the scratch. Now it was truly a problem for him.

This child was convinced that something awful would happen. He had read about people having to have amputations from tiny little scratches that they had neglected. Gangrene. Flesh-eating bacteria. Spiders that burrow into holes in your skin and eat you from the inside out. The best idea was to take precautions until Mom could clean things up. He didn't consider the duct tape an over-reaction. Although most of the world would have given this child a starring role in *Hypochondria: The Musical*, his mother knew exactly what neurological impulses had made him behave *in extremis*. Congratulations, fantastic mother of an NLDer, for your empathic performance, and for being able to retain your sense of humor through the emotional pain.

Are all NLDers, then, natural hypochondriacs? Absolutely not. People with hypochondria, a serious somatoform disorder, are preoccupied with imaginary illnesses and physical complaints. People with NLD merely see any physical problem that actually affects them in the worst possible light, using the classic black-or-white philosophy and pessimistic outlook by which they measure many other life events. Some even throw in a little of their natural propensity toward obsessive compulsive disorder (OCD) and think about the most repugnant and dire prognostic outcomes of whatever symptoms they might display. But what separates the NLDer from the hypochondriac is that NLDers usually don't start worrying until they have a real symptom, and they are quite capable of relinquishing the worry when the symptom is either (a) gone, or (b) explained with airtight logic in a manner which assures them of its natural limitations.

Another reason that causes people with NLD to be threatened by a physical problem or minor illness is that they are unable to assume a perspective outside of themselves. They retain an almost childlike self-centeredness – though not necessarily an egotistical self-centeredness – well into late adolescence and sometimes throughout their adult years. Moreover, the sudden transition from wellness into the mode of injury or illness can be quite unsettling to a person with NLD, who prefers to move gradually from one state of being to another.

Matters are complicated further by the fact that many people with NLD have difficulty expressing not only emotional states of wellbeing or distress, but also the ranges of feeling and intensity that describe physical conditions. Before my son was diagnosed with lactose intolerance as a young child, he was unable to describe more than a vague discomfort in the abdominal area. Other NLDers are unable to pinpoint even the general location of something that is bothering them. This inability to define something by its specific characteristics is completely disorienting for people with NLD, who like to ground themselves physically and emotionally with as many details as possible. It also makes it difficult for those who want to help them, since the lack of specificity can impede diagnosis.

Some NLDers are so out of touch with the sensors of pain and discomfort in their bodies that they are not aware of injury of illness until it reaches extreme proportions. Watch your child carefully for any change in routine or level of activity. Many parents who have taken a child with NLD to the doctor for vague complaints have been shocked to learn that their son or daughter has a broken leg or a strep throat, conditions that would cause neurotypical children to scream with pain.

When the necessity for medical procedures that they do not understand is added to the illness or injury, NLDers can approach a state of near meltdown. If the questions they ask to balance themselves are not answered, and if the sensations and experiences of treatment assault their sensory systems as well as their capacity for intellectual integration, they are likely to respond poorly. It is critically important to remember at these times that withdrawal is a purely neurological response to an overwhelming situation. Maladaptive reactions to illness or injury can be even more pronounced in NLDers whose fundamental sense of emotional security and self-esteem is precarious.

How can we protect our children from these complications without keeping them in germ-proof, injury-proof bubbles? The most valuable thing we can do for our NLDers is to "gray them up" (see Chapter 14). By teaching them that there is a world of reasonably viable existence between the polarities of black and white, we can help them understand that there are situations that are neither perfect solutions nor total disasters. Each time they recover without loss of limb from a scratch to the extremities, it is our responsibility to file the experience in our compendium of teachable moments. The next time a child is totally decompensating at the sight of blood or a black-and-blue mark, access the mental "previous injury file."

"Remember when you bumped into the wall at Uncle Farfel's house? Boy, you really got a big purple lump on your forehead that time! You looked like you had such a big brain it was popping right out of your skull. But I can't even tell where that was. It didn't leave a mark at all."

At this point, your child will probably head for the nearest mirror to examine your assessment for reliability and validity. Each time you pass the critical values analysis of the NLD population, you are adding a little bit of gray to their black-and-white lives.

"Hmmm," your child might begin to think, "I guess you can hurt yourself a little and recover with no residual loss. That time I was sure I would be left with permanent brain damage. Okay, I guess I can wait a few hours without a meltdown to see if I'm going to live through this incident."

Most of us who are actively involved with the lives of NLDers recognize them as innocent little angels with no ulterior motives. On rare occasions, however, an NLDer has been known to feign illness to avoid undesirable confrontations or responsibilities, to garner sympathy or support, or simply to create a situation which looks more valid than simple procrastination and can enlist the interest and concern of caregivers even beyond those in the immediate family. Many parents feel manipulated by their children's frequent default to the modality of illness, especially since NLDers are rarely able to define specific symptoms. In most cases, however, what looks like manipulation is merely a cover-up for something more serious, although probably less physical, that is bothering your NLDer. The more you approach each illness with concern, the less inclined your child will be to fabricate symptoms of illness for secondary purposes.

There is no way to know how many times you will have to remind your children that most people don't die of the minor scrapes and scratches gained from daily encounters with inanimate objects. You may succeed in convincing them after a few carefully placed reminders. It might take dozens of reminders. And for some, just when it seems you shouldn't have to say it one more time, it clicks. "Hey, Ma. I scraped my knee on the playground at school. The nurse put a band-aid on it, though, and some first aid cream. I think it'll be okay."

There are definitely more serious concerns than scratches that can cause medical problems for people with NLD, affecting the areas of physical as well as emotional health. Parents of children with NLD, educators, and healthcare providers who work with NLDers know that anxiety can be the most disabling attribute of this disorder. In fact, most of the suggestions in this book and many other treatises on the subject of helping NLDers are geared toward alleviating the anxiety that disables the smooth integration of diverse areas of the central nervous system and, consequently, their optimal daily functioning.

It is no surprise that constant anxiety and frustration can lead to depression. Depression, left untreated, can lead to unremitting pain and, ultimately, suicide. The literature shows that people with learning disabilities have a higher suicide rate than people without learning disabilities. This is certainly no surprise. I am sure that it would also show that people with bilateral bunions or any other condition of unresolved agony would also show a higher rate of depression and suicide. What concerns us, however, is that among the learning-disabled population, already flagged for higher rates of suicide, adolescents and young adults with NLD have the highest documented suicide rate of all.

It should be the goal of the pro-NLDer community to render this statistic, cited by Rourke in his early works (Rourke 1989, 1995), an anomaly of the past. With intervention, compassion, and understanding, there should be no reason for people with NLD to enter the dark tunnel of frustration, isolation, and depression. However, as we work to eradicate the legitimacy of this statistic, it is equally important to remember its validity. Every time we see NLDers who are not being given the academic, social, and behavioral supports so critical to their happiness, success, and productivity, each of us must take the ongoing and active responsibility to do whatever we can to rectify the situation. We are all aware of the historical consequences of assuming that it can't happen here. The fight to recognize NLD as a viable, alternative way of being begins in those of us who love and understand people with NLD.

Since we have such a monumental task ahead of us, we need to keep our NLDers in the best of health so that they can support and participate in our advocacy campaign. Since many NLDers have hypotonia (low muscle tone), it is important to recognize the health consequences which may accompany that condition so that we can prevent some from occurring and alleviate those that do.

Many children with NLD, and, in fact, many infants with a wide variety of neurological and central nervous system disorders, are born with hypotonia. The National Organization for Rare Diseases (NORD) defines congenital benign hypotonia (CBH) as a neuromuscular condition of unknown origin characterized by low muscle tone with unusual "floppiness" of muscles that may be apparent at birth or during the first months of life.

The good news is that this condition is nonprogressive. It generally does not worsen over time, and in fact, it tends to improve. Although it occasionally persists into adulthood, the effects of hypotonia can be severely diminished with the intervention of a skilled occupational therapist (OT). If you believe that your NLDer has low muscle tone and an official diagnosis of CBH has not been made, the first thing to do is consult your pediatrician for confirmation. Then find a terrific OT and get busy.

Some children with CBH have a predisposition to developing pneumonia when they have upper respiratory illness because their weak chest muscles make it difficult for them to cough strongly and effectively. Make sure that you don't let a cold develop into anything more ominous. Here again, your pediatrician and OT can be your child's best friends.

Frankly, OTs can do so much to help children with NLD that it would be wonderful if every family could keep one on retainer! But for those of us who don't live on Fantasy Island, its good enough to identify a practice of qualified therapists who are familiar with NLD to maintain an ongoing relationship with your NLDers, whether or not they have hypotonia. OTs can work with your family, school personnel, and extracurricular activity facilitators to help your children be aware of the most effective ways to gain control over their sensorimotor and visual-spatial problems.

In some cases, hypotonia can affect the ability to suck and swallow. If liquid or food goes down the trachea into the lungs instead of down the esophagus into the stomach, your child may be at risk for aspiration pneumonia. When combined with oral defensiveness, the entire issue of eating can become a problem where, once again, the seemingly omnipotent OT should be called upon for advice. Since hypotonia can also affect the production of speech, you might want to contact a speech and language pathologist (SLP) who can help you with these issues as well. Although these are not technically areas that would be categorized as illness, they fall under the general rubric of things that might affect a child who has NLD, and for that reason, are included in this chapter.

One last caveat about hypotonia and its ramifications. Although we have noted that it generally improves with age, remember that, as with all symptoms connected to NLD, it affects every child to a different degree. For some children, the condition persists well into the teenage years and even into adulthood. Some may develop scoliosis due to weak back muscles and others may develop abdominal hernias due to weak stomach muscles. All you need to do, as the parents of children with NLD, is be prepared. If your child needs medical care, remember to be honest with clarifications, explain everything in a logical, age-appropriate manner, and consider all of your child's sensory issues before you proceed with any medical visits or procedures.

Although dealing with medical professionals will be discussed in Chapter 12, it is important for parents and caregivers to know that NLD can appear in conjunction with several other syndromes. It is neither the cause nor the result of this group of disorders, but it is simply comorbid with several complex neurological disorders which affect people in ways that include, but are not limited to, the symptoms of NLD.

Children with the following congenital syndromes and adults and children with certain neurological disorders or post-traumatic conditions have been found to exhibit characteristics similar to those seen in the syndrome of NLD. *I cannot state strongly enough that not everyone with NLD has these conditions, nor is everyone with NLD predisposed to any of these conditions.* However, people with other conditions that affect the white matter of the brain, the myelin, or the central nervous system often present with disabilities similar to those associated with NLD. It is also important to remember that only preliminary studies have been done to assess the relationship between these disorders and NLD.

Discussed at great length by Byron Rourke (Rourke 1995), these disorders include: agenesis of the corpus callosum, Asperger Syndrome (AS) and other types of pervasive developmental disorder (PDD), congenital hypothyroidism, deLange Syndrome, Fetal Alcohol Syndrome, multiple sclerosis (MS), Hydrocephalus, Metachromatic Leukodystrophy, Neurofibromatosis, Prophylactic Treatment for Acute Lymphocytic Leukemia, Sotos Syndrome, Spina Bifida, Toxicant Induced Encephalopathy, Traumatic Brain Injury, Turner Syndrome, Velocardiofacial Syndrome (VCF), and Williams Syndrome.

The issue of illness and injury is important not only when the child with NLD is directly affected. Some of the difficulties these children suffer in decoding the experience occur with the same magnitude when illness or injury covers someone they love. In fact, because many are not able to be forthcoming with their feelings about events which may have had a deep impression on them, you may not know which type of misconceptions or fears your children are harboring. Approach the illness of others in the same way you would approach the illness of your NLDer. Make sure that your child has the age-appropriate information to understand what is happening to whoever is affected, and to whoever will be affected in the family.

It is always better to understand reality than to construct a fantasy based on fear and falsehood. As always, remember your child's assets and deficits before you embark on any course of enlightenment or explanation. If the illness of a family member will involve any sort of change in the life of the NLDer, be explicit. Assure your children that you have carefully considered their needs and that they have nothing to fear at the moment. You can draw some important conclusions about how to deal with illness in the family from the story related below. You can also draw on an incredible example to counteract those who say that children with NLD have a diminished capacity for empathy.

In one family, a well-loved aunt was stricken with a rare and highly malignant cancer at the young age of 36. The course of the illness was unremittingly negative, and she died in less than a year from the date of diagnosis, leaving three young children. Her nephew, who was still a year shy of his NLD diagnosis, was seven years old. Although details of the aunt's illness were not discussed graphically in front of her nieces and nephews, the main facts could not be disguised. The family grieved and life went on. The cousins grew, but their mother never returned. The youngest nephew used his excellent rote memory skills to remember that when you get cancer you die and your children don't have a mother.

The story does not end here. Five years later, when he was in seventh grade, the youngest nephew's own mother was diagnosed with cancer. Her tumor was much less invasive with a good prognosis after surgery and chemotherapy. In fact, things went so well that the family decided not to mention the word "cancer" to their youngest child, although the older ones were completely informed. This, of course, was a mistake. The youngest boy was told that his mother had to go into the hospital for an overnight procedure and would be back the next day. Things proceeded as planned. The boy avoided his mother when she returned. The mother believed that he was uncomfortable approaching her in the "sickroom" with medical accoutrements like drainage tubes and pill bottles.

Happily, the mother recuperated miraculously. Sadly, the boy had somehow realized that his mother had been diagnosed with cancer. He made the following calculation. "My mother has cancer and she will probably die. I depend on her a lot to translate my world for me. She fixes things that go wrong in school, drives me everywhere, and listens to me when I need to talk and talk and talk. Soon I will have no one to depend on so I have to learn to rely on myself. It will be easier if I start doing that right away."

The boy completely severed his relationship with his mother. He employed elective mutism for two full years. Though she continued to speak to him, he never spoke a word to her. He conversed in his normal laconic manner with other family members, but he protected himself from projected loss by refusing to acknowledge that he needed his mother's help to get along in life. Needless to say, hearts were broken during this time. Professionals were consulted, all to no avail. The boy began to exhibit symptoms of clinical depression, spending hours in his room staring at the ceiling, wearing all black, failing all classes.

As a last resort, his parents decided to send him on a two-week bicycle trip for young teenagers who all fit into the category of being "just a bit different." The boy's parents sent the counselors every resource on NLD that was available. They bought every accessory that could hang off a bicycle without immobilizing it. They sent their sedentary, uncoordinated son off for the two-week bike trip hoping that he wouldn't end up in a ditch on the first day. The boy called home and spoke to his father at the required times, relaying little or no information. Both parents were relieved to know that all limbs and organs remained in working order.

At the end of the tour, his mother drove to the airport to pick him up. He waved goodbye to his peers. Mom spoke to the counselors and they said that the NLDer had exhibited none of the symptoms she had so carefully explained to them. Moreover, he had taken upon himself the chore of cooking for the group each evening and had astonished them all with surprises like blueberry soup and Caesar salad. Probably, it was the other teens who were most astonished, but the counselors had adored it. The boy and his mother got into the car. She braced herself for the long, silent trip home.

To her great surprise, the boy talked non-stop for two hours. Two years of pent-up information cascaded from his mouth. When they got home, he told her that he had a gift for her since he had missed her birthday. She inspected this child from head to foot to see if perhaps she had mistakenly taken home someone else's boy, but under a mantle of dirt, he looked remarkably like the one she had dropped off several weeks before.

He walked into her study and handed her a book. "Sorry I couldn't wrap it," he apologized. The book was called *Ten Women Talk About their Survival from Cancer*. In a tiny bookstore on Cape Cod, he had undergone a massive dose of graying up. Apparently not everyone gets cancer and dies. Sheepishly, he held out his hand. "This comes with it, too," he said. Something heavy, round, and flat was wrapped in wrinkled tissue paper. The boy's mother took the gift and opened it slowly, not knowing what to expect. In her palm lay a thick, coin-shaped piece of green glass. Through her tears, she could hardly read the word engraved on it – "Miracle." This time the boy let her hug him. He hugged back. Both arms. Not ready for a kiss yet, but they could always negotiate that tomorrow.

Key points

1. NLDers are not all natural hypochondriacs. Most, however, see any physical problem that actually affects them in the worst possible light, using the classic black-or-white philosophy and pessimistic outlook by which they measure many other life events. Most NLDers will relinquish their fears when the symptom is either (a) gone, or (b) explained with airtight logic in a manner which assures them of its natural limitations.

2. Some NLDers are unaware of physical pain and may suffer injury or illness without being aware of the seriousness of their condition.

3. Most NLDers feel threatened by physical problems or minor illness because they are unable to assume a perspective outside of themselves. They can also become unsettled by the sudden transition from wellness into the mode of injury or illness.

4.   Many children with NLD are born with hypotonia, a neuromuscular condition characterized by low muscle tone with unusual "floppiness" of muscles that may be apparent at birth or during the first months of life. Great strides to correct this condition can be made with interventional occupational therapy.

5.   For children with NLD, most things in the world fall neatly into two categories, good or bad. When they are injured or ill, it is important to help them understand why most conditions, though definitely on the negative side of good, are not 100 per cent bad, and most likely not fatal.

6.   People with learning disabilities have a higher suicide rate than neurotypicals, but adolescents and young adults with NLD have the highest documented suicide rate in the entire learning-disabled population. With the proper intervention and treatment, this statistic can become a bad memory in the ancient history of NLD.

Chapter Twelve
Medical Appointments

Children with NLD do not usually require more medical care than neurotypical children, although occasionally they must undergo batteries of educational, psychological, neuropsychological, or neurological testing which are less than enjoyable experiences for their sensorimotor systems. However, during the course of even the healthiest, most normal childhoods, it is incumbent upon parents to take their children to a series of well child checkups. We must assure ourselves that developmental milestones, both physical and emotional, are being met within a few standard deviations of recommended norms. In addition, the marvels of civilization have given us the opportunity to enjoy excellent eyesight, long-term dental health, and a wealth of other medical advantages for which previous generations had no markers and no interventions. To do so, however, requires the attention and intervention of carefully trained specialists and the tools of their trades.

Progress is generally a good thing. Fluoride treatments from an early age prevent our children from having to withstand the noxious whirring of the dentist's drill as he or she bores cavernous chasms into sensitive dental enamel and then adds insult to injury by filling the holes with the worst-tasting concoction ever inserted into a human mouth. But procedures that are mildly annoying to neurotypical kids, even when they ultimately forestall procedures that could be much worse, can be devastatingly difficult for

children with NLD. A visit to the dentist can seem like an endless struggle against sensory sensitivity. A visit to the ophthalmologist can feel like a forced foray through the Tunnel of Horror. A well-meaning pediatrician with a "How about them Giants?" personality can send an NLDer into repulsion convulsions.

Fortunately, to use an expression that many NLDers would have trouble interpreting literally, forewarned is forearmed. When you know what types of places, personalities, and procedures stress your NLDer, you can take precautions to make sure that you minimize interaction with them. Whatever the specialty, choose your healthcare provider with extreme caution. Don't assume that every pediatrician knows about NLD. Unfortunately, more don't than do. Before you even think about making an appointment, you have a lot of work to do. If you want your child to be fairly comfortable in a doctor's office, you must learn to be an aggressive consumer when interviewing potential practitioners.

Ask if the physicians in the office you will be visiting regularly see children with pervasive developmental disorders. Ask what they have read on the subject and how up to date they are on the latest professional literature. Find out if they network with other practitioners who see children with NLD to learn what approaches work best and what might exacerbate sensory defensiveness or anxiety. Talk to the doctor about the centers closest to you geographically which do research and treat children with neurological disorders. Is this pediatrician affiliated with the researchers or physicians there? After you ask your NLD-specific questions, speak to the office manager about the normal procedure of an office visit. Is there usually a long wait, even if you have an appointment? Who will see your child in the event of an emergency, or if the physician who treats your child is away?

Go to the actual office where your child will be seen if you become a patient. What does the space look like? Is there an area where a child could retreat and listen to music or read a book, or is there general chaos with toys on the floor and babies bawling and crawling? What is the overall sensory message that you receive from the office? Is it hectic and filled with stimuli or is it calming and quiet?

Magnify your impressions tenfold to try to imagine how your NLDer might react to the ambience and décor. Remember to keep your NLDer's specific assets and deficits in mind. If fluorescent lighting is a factor which causes instant meltdown in your NLDer, an office with that type of lighting will probably never feel comfortable. If noise is your child's specific bugaboo, make sure to find a practice where there is a quiet corner or where the doctor will allow your child to wait in an exam room instead of joining the waiting room circus.

As difficult as it may seem to choose a pediatrician for children with NLD, choosing a dentist is even more complex. Fear of the dentist and dental procedures is common even in the neurotypical population. Approximately 30–40 million Americans are so afraid of dental treatment that they avoid it altogether. If this is the magnitude of fear in a population not known for oral defensiveness and heightened anxiety, imagine what the statistics would show if we polled the NLD population for their opinion of the overall dental experience.

Since my family and I have been lucky enough to find a dentist who treats us with utmost professionalism, poise, sensitivity, and even a sense of humor, I believe that it is possible for others to find a similar standard of excellence. Of course, all the questions that you asked about pediatricians apply. Although it's not important that your dentist be intimately acquainted with the specific details of the latest NLD research, it is necessary that he or she be aware of the responses of children with neurological, developmental disorders and, most important, with the responses of children with disorders of sensory integration.

Many parents who consult me about their children's refusal to comply with what most of the civilized world considers minimal hygiene bemoan the fact that they cannot seem to help their children understand the need to brush their teeth with any schedule that approaches regularity. Some have gone so far as to ask if children with NLD are inherently unsanitary. Actually, if anything, the reverse is true. But their unwillingness to follow the American Dental Association's optimal brushing and flossing guidelines stems once again from that complicated system of tangled responses – the dysfunction of sensory integration.

Every adult with NLD discussing this topic recalls a period when certain toothpastes were intolerable because of taste or a sensation of actual stinging. Some had the same reactions to mouthwash or to the bristles of different toothbrushes. Since most were young children when these reactions first occurred, they had neither the language nor the understanding to say to their parents, "Let's try every type of toothpaste and bristle until we find the combination that is most comfortable." One young adult with NLD sports a clean and healthy smile today which belies the fact that for a period of a year she simply ran her toothbrush under water each morning to delude her mother into believing she had brushed her teeth. When her family inadvertently started buying another brand of toothpaste, she had the courage to try once again and has been brushing happily ever since.

Following a serious program of dental care at home is, of course, one way to minimize lengthy interactions with the dentist. When such visits can't be avoided, however, try to help your child understand that the dentist will have to stand quite close in order to work effectively. Arrange with your dentist before each appointment to develop a signal that your child can use to indicate "Stop! You absolutely must move away right now." Explain that your child might become disoriented when asked to move his face to the right or to the left, so it is better to say, "Move your head toward the plant," or even to guide the child's chin gently if that has been agreed upon beforehand as an acceptable touch.

If your child can't stand the sound of the instruments, bring music. If the lights are bothersome, bring sunglasses. Find out what new "toys" your dentist has to take your child's mind off of the dental work. At a recent root canal appointment, an experience never high on my favorite activity list, my dentist let me choose a movie to watch on a special headset which did not interfere with her access to my mouth. As soon as I got involved in the escapades onscreen, I forgot to remember that I hate the sound of the drill, hate the feeling of the rubber dam, and hate the taste of the amalgam. In fact, I stayed for 20 minutes longer just to see the end of the movie.

Even with every precaution you can imagine, and others that astonishingly creative parents devise, some children with NLD still remain extremely uncomfortable about seeing the dentist for regular checkups and especially for more invasive dental work. Although parents, and especially those who are not physicians by profession, are not required to take the Hippocratic oath, most do live by its theoretical foundation where their children are concerned – first, do no harm. So if you have children who simply cannot overcome their fear of the dentist, discuss the possibility of mild, short-acting sedation or anti-anxiety medication with your pediatrician and dentist. Some children need to use such pharmaceutical intervention only once or twice until they realize that they have undergone dental treatment and have survived. For others, it is a lifelong addendum to the dental experience.

When choosing an ophthalmologist for children with NLD, it is important to find a practitioner who understands the differences between vision and visual-spatial function and who has at least a primary knowledge of the way NLD can affect visual perception. Since approximately one child in four has a vision disorder that can interfere with the ability to learn, it is important for parents who are already aware that their child might have visual-spatial deficits to choose an eye doctor who can literally and figuratively see the entire picture.

Children with NLD can pass a standard vision test with a flawless score of 20/20, because routine eye exams do not test for visual imagery and visual memory. The routine test may also be unable to inform parents and educators that a child is unable to copy information from the blackboard or to make sense of instructions written on a homework assignment sheet that is festooned with smiley faces and cutesy graphics. However, it is important to identify early what situations help your child feel most comfortable in school.

By describing the assets and deficits common to the NLD syndrome, you may be able to guide your ophthalmologist toward a more thorough examination of your child's specific strengths and weaknesses. Through awareness, and the appropriate accommodations which follow, we can help our children avoid struggling with assignments in class, spending excessive and frustrating hours on homework, and ultimately avoiding schoolwork that taxes their visual-spatial difficulties.

Within the community of children with learning disabilities and those who seek to help them, there is a group of parents who are devoted to the services of developmental optometrists and the practice of a modality called *vision therapy*. Some developmental optometrists examine children who are having problems in school and recommend exercises to treat conditions such as "deficient eye teaming," "tracking problems," or problems with "visual memory." Many parents of NLDers attest to the success of vision therapy and to the sustained accomplishments of their children after treatment.

I consider it important to give the position on vision therapy held by the American Academy of Pediatrics (AAP), the American Academy of Ophthalmology (AAO), and the American Association for Pediatric Ophthalmology and Strabismus (AAPOS). Their joint position paper on vision therapy (AOA 1997) states that, although a thorough ophthalmic examination is recommended to determine whether glasses are necessary or not, vision therapy is not recommended because, "There is no known eye or visual cause for these learning disabilities and no known effective visual treatment." Granting that no harm can be done from vision therapy, they note that it is nevertheless important to get an accurate diagnosis and begin appropriate treatment and remediation promptly rather than invest time and money in a therapy which has not been proven medically effective.

Although the ophthalmologist you choose should not be expected to actively participate in the educational remediation of a patient, he or she should be able to provide optimal professional eye care and then direct the family to the appropriate professional best able to undertake the task of helping these children learn most efficiently. By having a "feel" for the subject, your doctors can provide the first step in directing the family where to get the best help available. Ideally, the ophthalmologist and other physicians involved with your child should work together with the neuropsychologist to coordinate diagnosis and remediation at school as well as interventions in other realms of life.

We all know that every child with NLD has a unique combination of assets and deficits. By helping the medical practitioners who treat our children understand each unique profile, we can guarantee the kind of medical attention that will make our children optimally comfortable. It would be decidedly counterproductive to make an appointment for your child without personally investigating the facilities and the caregivers.

The recommendation of another parent might not give you all the information you need to assess the situation appropriately for your own child's particular needs. After you have visited the office and spoken with the healthcare provider, it is a good idea to send a letter describing your child to be kept with other medical records. Ask that the doctor make everyone involved in your child's care, including office receptionists, nurses, and other healthcare assistants, aware of your child's specific assets, deficits, preferences, and needs. Even a superstar can't excel without a supporting team!

The letter you send to a medical office should be inclusive and factual, but should not be a running commentary of deficits. Include some of your child's positive characteristics and describe some special personality details. Make the physician and staff look forward to the arrival of their new patient and feel privileged to be part of your child's healthcare team.

Here is a sample of a letter for an ophthalmologist:

Dear Dr. Oculus,

My son, Icarus Bullfinch, is looking forward to his eye examination next week because he loves to read and wants to make sure that his "equipment" is in tip-top shape for first grade. Before we come in, however, I wanted to let you know that Icarus has been diagnosed with a neurological syndrome called nonverbal learning disorder (NLD) which may affect certain responses during his eye exam. If he refuses to do something you ask, he is not being intentionally difficult or oppositional. I hope the following points will help you keep both yourself and Icarus comfortable and happy in your office.

1.   Icarus may have problems with direction. It helps to gently show him the direction instead of just asking him to turn right or left.

2.   Icarus may react to certain procedures with hypersensitivity. Changes to darkness or bright light may disorient him momentarily. Please believe him when he tells you what he can tolerate and what he cannot.

3.   Icarus is an auditory learner. If you explain exactly what you are doing, he will be much more comfortable with any procedure.

4.   If Icarus fails to respond when you use a nonverbal gesture, such as pointing, try using oral directions to see if he can comply.

5.   The syndrome of NLD can cause deficits in visuospational reasoning. Please make sure that you help us understand

Icarus's visual function beyond the realm of simple vision acuity.

6. Icarus may withdraw if he believes he is about to be touched. His sensory defensiveness does not allow him to respond openly to casual touch. If touching him is part of the examination, for example when it is necessary to use eye-drops, you can help him get ready by explaining why you must hold his head or chin.

As you may have guessed from our child's name, Mr. Bullfinch and I are great fans of ancient mythology. However, we did not anticipate the cruelty of other children when we chose our first-born's name. We ask that you be sensitive and not try to use a nickname. He enjoys being called Icarus, but shrinks into a posture of negative unrest when called "Icky."

Thanks in advance for agreeing to be part of Icarus's medical team. He is a bright and interesting child with an advanced vocabulary, many interests, and a wonderful heart. I have enclosed a short article on NLD as well as a bibliography should you be inclined to delve further into the subtleties of this low-incidence learning disability.

Sincerely,

Athena Bullfinch

The sample letter can be adapted not only to the specialty of whatever practitioner your child must see, but also to the specific behaviors your child has been known to present. If you are aware that some procedures which are necessary elements of certain medical disciplines are meltdown triggers for your child, it would be wise to discuss this beforehand or to mention it in a letter. Some procedures must remain as they are, but others can be modified and still produce the same results. For example, many immunizations can only be administered by injection, which may cause some children to lose all sensory composure. A physician who is aware of this possibility, however, can apply a numbing cream early in the examination to the area where your child must receive the injection. By the time the syringe looms, the injection will cause only 10 percent of the normal sensory reaction. In most cases, 10 percent of a meltdown is much preferred to the full show.

Parents must remember that not every physician or healthcare provider has the skills or personality to work with children who have NLD. Even the most mildly affected child exhibits some cognitive inflexibility and occasional difficulty with self-monitoring skills. Some very competent professionals can become frustrated when working with patients who have NLD. They are then unable to get to the heart of medical matters because they are diverted by superficial behaviors. These are not the right professionals for your child. It may take several attempts to get a good fit, but careful investigation is the only way to insure that you and your child enjoy beneficial results.

Key points

1. Don't assume that every physician or healthcare provider knows about NLD. Unfortunately, more don't than do. If you want your child to be fairly comfortable in a doctor's office, you must learn to be an aggressive consumer when interviewing potential practitioners. Before you even think about making an appointment, you must make sure that you learn everything about the doctor and the doctor's office, while simultaneously making sure that the doctor knows as much as possible about your NLDer.

2. Write a description of specific assets and deficits to be kept on file with your child's medical records. Ask that the doctor make everyone involved in your child's care, including office receptionists, nurses, and other healthcare assistants, aware of your child's specific preferences and needs.

3. Children with NLD can be calmed before medical appointments by being told what to expect at what is an age-appropriate level for them. They can also be very helpful in figuring out effective interventions, such as sunglasses to deflect bright light in the dental chair.

4. When investigating alternative therapies, make sure that they can do no harm and that they do not make extravagant claims for miraculous remediation. Every branch of medicine has a regulating body which can direct you to reliable and valid research.

Chapter Thirteen

Friends

Although most of us no longer wear granny glasses, bell bottoms, and nehru jackets, the memory of John Lennon singing "I get by with a little help from my friends" is still fundamental to the social philosophy of the generation raising the first cohort of children formally diagnosed with nonverbal learning disorders. We live in a global village where conviviality is prized and isolation is suspect. In fact, foreign policy and fundamentalism have taken the word "alienation" far from its original meaning of emotional distance. It is now the mark of the social deviant, a suspicious loner or pariah. In modern times, good parents are not necessarily those who raise their children to be moral, intellectual, thoughtful, or generous. The good parents of the twenty-first century are those who raise their children to be popular.

The social whirl starts early. Most infants begin going to playgroups as soon as they leave the nursery. Once thought to be genial gatherings for new mothers who really couldn't get out much, playgroups have become evaluative social skill sessions where anxious parents of neonates evaluate the oblivious occupants of infant seats for reciprocal gaze, returned smile reflex, and intensity of interpersonal involvement. Mothers develop social resumés and sophisticated expecta-

tions for creatures whose greatest discovery is that it is great fun to stick your big toe into your mouth.

Ironically, most of these babies are contented unless they are hungry, tired, or in pain. As soon as these fundamental problems are alleviated, they go back to their primary developmental task – keeping themselves happy. The scholarly literature of early childhood has never described infants or toddlers who went out of their way to make others happy. Nevertheless, they are inherently designed to do so, with their chubby cheeks and irresistible smiles. Thus equipped, they guarantee that no one cares if their perspective is purely egocentric. It works for them and it works for the people who love them. Babies are born superstars, but they must struggle for the rest of their lives to maintain that distinction.

As children grow, however, and begin to leave the house in conveyances other than infant carriers, their social world and social perspective expand as well. Neurotypical children easily absorb assurances of appreciation, in verbal and nonverbal ways, from their family members and caregivers. Children who are unable to read the nonverbal signals, however, may not develop enough confidence in certain social interactions to initiate them voluntarily.

Ultimately, children must learn to juggle the elements of social cognition in order to participate effectively in the game of childhood friendships, whether in the toddler playgroup, or at the adolescent malt shop. Discussing children who are more challenging to raise than others, Greenspan reminds us that children processing incoming signals from peers must react rapidly to multiple sensations at the same time (Greenspan 1995). He stresses that inflections, nuance, nonverbal signals, or humor may be more important than information conveyed in a straight verbal manner. As the parents of children with NLD, we know that they traditionally struggle with multiple sensations, nonverbal communication, and complex motor activities. Does this mean that they must automatically forfeit the possibility of childhood friendships?

I am reminded of a classic episode of *I Love Lucy*, during which the forlorn comedienne sits on a park bench, thinking she has been abandoned by all of her friends. She is approached by an organization remarkably similar in dress and mission to the Salvation Army, calling themselves the Friends of the Friendless. Tears streaming down her face as she recalls how her nearest and dearest have forgotten her, Lucy joins the ragtag band as they march, beat the drum, and sing, "We're the Friends of the Friendless…" On *I Love Lucy,* everything ends happily, because her friends have only been pretending to exclude her while they plan a surprise party in her honor. But for children with NLD, and even more so for adolescents, things do not always end as neatly as they do on a television sitcom.

Since children with NLD are usually unable to decipher the nuances of peer relationships, they evaluate friendships on the black-and-white spectrum that serves as their default for assessing so many of life's challenges. Struggling to understand the expectations of others, NLDers often erase the bloom of friendship before the bud is even set. They don't realize classmates might not be comfortable being considered someone's best friend when their only shared activity was having lunch together on a field trip. Similarly, children don't respond well to someone who phones them excessively or is annoyingly omnipresent in a relationship. Some NLDers display extremely passive behavior in relationships and risk becoming the pawns of exploitative peers. Others simply don't understand the concept of compromise, and lose potential friends who are overwhelmed by the NLDer's domination of activities, conversations, and relationship rules.

Throughout my three decades of motherhood, my children have been trying to teach me that if *I* am cold, *they* don't have to put on sweaters. I am very close to learning that lesson, although I don't think I'm quite ready for the final exam. Nevertheless, I like to think that if I believed that children with NLD could truly be happy without friends, I would not impose my extraverted, gregarious preferences on them. In many conversations with young NLDers, however, I have learned that many are frustrated and some even heartbroken by their difficulties in interpreting the social code. In the domain of social cognition, parents and caregivers must remain actively involved to help children with NLD develop and utilize the basic rules of social interaction.

In the earlier years of a child's life, parents control the social schedule and arrange play dates. A parent usually accompanies a three- or four-year-old child to the social engagement, and the adults schmooze and supervise while their little geniuses engage in parallel play and take notice of each other only when there is just one cookie left on the snack table. By kindergarten and the early years of elementary school, however, children become more discriminating about their social engagements. Although they are not yet interested in someone with whom they can exchange therapeutic revelations, they like to visit friends who have similar interests (i.e. good toys) and values (i.e. a heated indoor pool or a mom who bakes cookies from scratch).

By the middle elementary years, that elusive concept of "cool" creeps into peer relationships and definitely puts children with NLD at a disadvantage. Most NLDers are amply endowed with integrity, kindness, diligence, and fairness, but they usually come up short in the category of cool. Suddenly Obadiah is shunned even though he has a more amazing collection of fully intact shed snakeskins than most professional herpetologists. The girls giggle at Victoria behind her back because she's not comfortable wearing trendy short skirts and rickety high heels to school. The lines have been drawn, and unfortunately, most NLDers find themselves alone on a team of one.

Even when NLDers of elementary and early middle school age do succeed in encouraging classmates or neighborhood children to come over, they are often unable to sustain mutual activity. Although the afternoon may begin promisingly, mothers or fathers trying to supervise unobtrusively find out soon that the NLDer is doing what he or she wants and the invited guest is trying to find ways to remain occupied while wondering how long it will be before a parent's car pulls up in the driveway for liberation.

Many NLDers say that they would like to have friends from their peer group, but simply do better with younger children they can commandeer or older people who are intrigued by their eccentricities and interests. Most are not antisocial, but rather are simply unaware of the responsibilities of entertaining a guest or of keeping another's perspective in mind for several hours. Young guests who have been bored and ignored for a visit or two rarely accept a return invitation.

After being systematically rebuffed by a number of, if not all, children in their class, NLDers begin to stop initiating friendships. They protect themselves from rejection by pretending that they'd rather be alone, and turn toward inward activities that can activate or enhance depression. Some NLDers respond to rejection by becoming bullies. Rather than let others make fun of them, they choose to take the offensive. Whether in a passive, passive-aggressive, or purely aggressive mode, an NLDer who claims to be comfortable in isolation is rarely telling the whole story.

So what can parents and caregivers do to enhance healthy relationships in childhood and early adolescence for children with NLD? The first thing is to remember that most NLDers are auditory learners. Make sure that they hear you describe the advantages of your relationships and friendships in great detail. Tell them how a visit to a museum with a friend helped you understand something from a new and different perspective. Discuss stories from the news and media about friendship. Build a shelf in the NLD perspectives closet about mutually beneficial relationships. As your child gets older, he or she may begin to realize that there are some advantages in letting others into your world, even if you have to make some little changes in the way you generally do things.

One NLDer I know quite well talked non-stop from the time he was 11 months old until he began middle school. Then his monologues and questions gradually dwindled until he barely spoke at all. One might think that his family would have enjoyed the respite, but actually his withdrawal distressed them and they ultimately brought their child to a therapist. In time, he revealed to the therapist that he avoids initiating a conversation because the signals that result from its continuation are often confusing and difficult to interpret. By the time he was 15, he had concluded, unfortunately, that it was just easier not to talk to people at all unless absolutely necessary.

Situations like these remind us that NLD, although technically relegated to the realm of learning disability, is actually a social-cognitive developmental disorder which can affect every aspect of your child's life 24 hours a day. Although some learning differences are limited to school time and homework, NLD is pervasive, requiring parents and caregivers to pay careful attention to all behaviors and explanations for behavior. When a child with NLD says, "Oh, I really prefer spending quiet time in my room. I don't like having friends over after school," make sure you find out why. It may be a healthy, self-soothing mechanism to decompensate from all the pressure and sensory stimulation of a day at school. On the other hand, it could be a pathological retreat from the world of interpersonal relations based on fear and anxiety.

As your child gets older, there are many types of social cognitive therapy that are effective for some children and young adolescents with NLD. Although many critics of social skills groups say that the behaviors learned there do not generalize to real-world, independently occurring situations, some NLDers can ultimately reduce anxiety by learning that it's all right to make mistakes and that no one expects every response or social behavior to be perfect. This helps them realize that the perfectly scripted social encounters they see on television or in the movies are completely fictional. Even superstars can stutter, fumble, or simply say, "Huh?"

As children get older, they may begin to articulate their frustration about difficulties with social interaction. This is a good time to start discussing the problem of perspective taking and NLD. Once NLDers can accept the concept that other people might feel more comfortable being included in a conversation or activity, they can take steps to correct their natural proclivities. They need to understand that not all people would be mesmerized to learn, for example, that the dominant female in a band of marmosets actually makes her subordinates infertile: Their ovaries shrivel and stop releasing eggs. The NLDer who is immensely interested in this odd little creature might monologue for hours without realizing that most listeners had long since passed on (or out) to wild monkey dreams. These monologues usually diminish in length, if not in frequency, as NLDers begin to realize that other people suddenly find themselves in need of the powder room when certain subjects recur.

Since NLDers have difficulty interpreting social cues and gestures, they may not know that they are overstepping the bounds of boredom if they are imposing upon a particularly polite listener. Despite the fact that the receiver of the fascinating esoterica is rolling his eyes, shuffling his feet, grimacing, and wringing his hands, the dauntless NLDer may continue describing the patina on the Statue of Liberty's nose, layer by layer. However, an NLDer who has had some instruction in social cognition, though unable to read the cues intuitively, may recall being told to look for a list of behaviors which indicate that sponsorship has been rescinded for the show. Perhaps a second or two later than a neurotypical might respond, he will change the topic. A carefully trained observer might notice a lag in response time, but most people would assume that the NLDer was just being reflective.

Friendship, even for neurotypical adults, is a complex procedure. For children and adolescents with NLD, it is a situation that is almost impossible to manage intuitively, or alone. As long as your help doesn't overpower the possibility of any true friendship ever developing, it is perfectly acceptable to do things for your NLDer that wouldn't be age-appropriate for a neurotypical peer. You can make a call to arrange a meeting, buy two tickets for an event you know your child will like and suggest that a classmate might come along, or call a sympathetic parent and ask to "accidentally" meet somewhere with your kids. Remember that all of the skills which are difficult for NLDers to develop are those which cement the bonds of friendship. No one can become a superstar if he can't get a ride to the game.

NLDers with visual-spatial impairment can't read visual cues that others give them and probably won't be good at team sports, an activity where many friendships are forged. Those who have trouble with executive function might be impulsive, unable to associate consequences with actions, and unable to follow multistep directions. Although some classmates might actually find the latter set of behaviors endearing, most class parents would not. Add to this the tendency to fixate on their own interests, over-react when asked to change plans, and be extremely picky about new experiences and places, and it becomes no surprise that NLDers are generally considered high-maintenance companions to cultivate.

But even though children with NLD seem to be several years less mature in the realm of social relationships than their peers, you will notice that one day, there is no standing too close, talking too loud, or trying to make friends through displays of inappropriate or disruptive behaviors. Everything will have come together in its own way at its own pace. Your NLDer will be able to cultivate friendships according to the special needs and dictates of the syndrome of NLD. They may not be the friendships you have dreamed about, but neither will they be the nightmares of isolation and ostracism which have startled you at night. Remember to praise your NLDers when you see them responding appropriately to the perspectives and needs of other people. This will motivate a recurrence of the behavior, even if the motivation seems apparent only to you.

Yet who are we to say that a child with NLD needs friends if he or she attests that it is more comfortable to be alone? Well, there are many philosophies in the religious and spiritual realm which sanctify friendship, and anyone who has ever enjoyed the pleasures of true friendship does not need scholarly justification for encouraging it. But in the 1950s, Harry Stack Sullivan, the guru of early developmental psychology, said that friendships enable children to acquire interpersonal sensitivity, learn new social skills, and receive validation in relationships (Sullivan 1953). Clearly, then, children without friends lack these avenues for developing the interactive fluency necessary for productive adult life. In exploring the friendship patterns of children with and without learning disabilities, Judith Wiener and Barry Schneider validated the theory that helping a socially rejected child with learning disabilities to enhance a friendship with another potentially compatible child may be a useful intervention modality, one that is perhaps more realistic than social skills intervention aimed at peer acceptance in groups (Wiener and Schneider 2002).

Once again, it is the primary relation of parent or caregiver to child which can make the difference between raising a happy NLDer who is interactive in a genuine and reflective manner, and sheltering a depressed and alienated loner who will always remain outside the window looking in. Talk about the benefits of friends and relationships at the dinner table or in the car. In age-appropriate doses, allow your children to spend a few moments mingling with guests at your house parties. Let them see how much fun people who care about each other can have together. Use examples in television shows, movies, and books to show how enriching relationships can be. Be a friend and model the richness of such relationships to your NLD children. There are some children who are truly antisocial, but that is generally the result of a personality disorder, not NLD. Think of friendship for the NLDer in a musical metaphor. You may be inherently musical but if no one teaches you how to read the notes and use your hands correctly, you will never be able to play the piano. Even the child who is not destined to be a virtuoso can learn to put together a few pleasing measures with practice.

The art of friendship for NLDers has a down side, too, and we, as their caretakers, must make sure that they are never harmed or negatively affected by predatory relationships. There will always be people waiting to exploit others. NLDers are known to be trusting and innocent, and some are ideal prey for rapists, thieves, and other unsavory types. Most children today are savvy enough to run from strangers and not to believe information they get from strangers. But even a highly intelligent NLDer is likely to believe information received from a stranger in a convincing auditory delivery. Confronted with a scene like this, most would run to tell the teacher or principal. But Irving would probably thank his future tormentor and get right into the car. It's not that Irving is stupid. He simply doesn't have the neuro-logical wiring to be critical or judgmental in this situation.

"Come on, Irving, I'm sorry I'm late. Your mother had an emergency errand today and she asked me to pick you up for her."

"Okay," Irving would respond as he got into the stranger's car. His mother would probably appear a minute or two later and begin to shriek. But Irving would sit unaware with the stranger until his evil doings became patently clear.

Don't leave Irving alone. Be his friend. Remember:

> A true friend is someone who thinks that you are a good egg even though he knows that you are slightly cracked.

> *(Meltzer 1982)*

Key points

1. You can enhance the ability of your NLDer to make and keep friends by remembering that most NLDers are auditory learners. Describe the advantages of your relationships and friendships in great detail and discuss stories from the media about friendship. Stress the benefits of relationship so that your child will have reasons to overcome fear and anxiety in initiating social interaction.

2. NLDers rarely prefer isolation. Those who choose this lifestyle are usually protecting themselves from rejection by pretending that they'd rather be alone.

3. Turning toward inward activities can activate or enhance depression, which is the greatest enemy of productivity and independence.

4. Teach your child to discriminate among levels of reliability in auditory information.

5. Not everything everyone says is always true.

6. Help your child understand the concept of compromise and the awareness of the perspectives of others. This will build a theoretical foundation on which positive social interaction and friendship can be based.

Chapter Fourteen

Graying Them Up: The Stages between Black and White

There are many colors between the two extremes of black and white. The sad thing is that children with NLD, unless they are carefully exposed to the splendors of the spectrum, never see or acknowledge anything but the polar opposites. Like many of the attributes of this complex syndrome, the NLDer's tendency to interpret situations as either black or white has both assets and deficits. Because they accept what is said as valid, they rarely understand or engage in personal manipulation or deception. Unless there are specific circumstances which they are unable to integrate into their particular awareness of self, they are uncompromisingly honest. But for the same reason, they are uncompromisingly gullible, clearly a deficit in modern society.

Whatever the benefits, categorizing people, events, and emotions as either black or white cuts off a range of possibilities which might make certain situations more tolerable and emotional reactions less difficult to endure. As we have mentioned, in the minds of NLDers who have not been exposed to shades of gray, the only tools for classification are "good" or "bad." So when such children take a test in school and get one answer wrong, they become extremely upset and assume that they have done badly.

They conclude logically that, since something with a mistake is flawed, it must be bad. The idea of relative gradations of good and bad has to be carefully and systematically introduced, since at first it seems like an illogical concept to a person with NLD.

In Chapter 2, we discussed the fact that people with NLD process information primarily with the left brain. Whether for genetic, congenital, or post-traumatic reasons, this means that people with NLD do not share information between the right and left hemispheres. Although the two hemispheres may look almost identical on physical examination, scientists have spent years studying the specific areas of function which are governed by each hemisphere. The brain is so highly specialized that not only are hemispheres categorized, even the folds have functions. The left hemisphere, which usually remains highly serviceable in NLDers, controls logic, reasoning, and analytical thought. It focuses clearly on details.

Unfortunately, it is the right hemisphere which helps the brain organize the details into an understanding of the whole picture, or *gestalt*. This explains why NLDers have problems seeing intermediate possibilities when trying to understand the classification of an event, emotion, or action. They analyze only the details – took a test, made a mistake, obvious conclusion = the result was not good. If NLDers had been able to use the right brain for simultaneous analysis, they might have been able to conclude, "Yes, I did take a test and make a mistake, but I only got one wrong. I really knew almost all of the material for that test, and received one of the highest grades in my class. I should be very proud of myself for this achievement."

When you begin to point out to a person with NLD that a test with one wrong answer is not exactly considered a failure, you will probably feel as though you are having a discussion with a brick wall. Very little will be absorbed, and after a while, you may develop quite a headache. But if you use every opportunity you can to demonstrate the valid reality between black and white, your NLDer might gradually begin to consider these possibilities. NLDers are notoriously hard on themselves because they are not aware that the possibility to be gentle exists. If you help them understand this possibility, you can reduce anxiety, raise self-esteem, and eliminate the self-defeating attitude that prevents NLDers from trying new things.

It's easier to begin this process with things that are measurable or quantifiable. Big, bigger, biggest is a lot easier to learn than good, better, best. But after practicing on easy things – such as, Cedric had a big helping of cookies, but Rupert's was bigger – move on to slightly less quantifiable occurrences. "Wasn't that an enormous rain storm last night? Much bigger than the drizzle we had this morning."

The next step, of course, is to discuss things that aren't really measurable at all. "Chauncey is a good friend. He gave me the code to the Medieval Elfmen Tree-Dweller Vigilante Video Game. But I think I like Angora even better. She comes over to visit and plays the game with me. That's a lot of fun." So Chauncey is a good friend, but Angora is a better friend.

Graying up is not important for school alone. The inability to see things in varied levels of intensity is a pervasive deficit of the syndrome of NLD. Social and emotional perceptions are all distorted by the difficulty in acknowledging that the situation could look different through a neuro-typical lens. All social interactions, in fact, are affected by the way a child learns to understand the social cognitive skills with which he must address his peers.

The difficulty that NLDers face in naming and describing their own emotions is a problem that continues both in school and out, in relation-ships, in groups, or even when they are alone.

> The ability to diagnose group dynamics helps children to develop cognitive and social skills that will be very valuable in school – and beyond school into the real world… They learn that most of life operates in shades of gray, not in all-or-nothing extremes. Sizing up these subtle shades of gray requires understanding that feelings and relationships can exist in relative terms. A child begins to learn that "I can be a little mad one day, a lot mad the next day, and furious on still another day."
>
> *(Greenspan 1995, p.25)*

The message of perfection that our children interpret from even the most ingenuous remarks in the world around them is another source of unremit-ting anxiety. A teacher who innocently tells the kids in class to go home and do a fantastic job on their homework can send a child with NLD into the throes of terror and despair. "Fantastic" is a difficult term to categorize, but for NLDers, it seems to fit into the default area of "perfect." How many of us have seen our children spending hours on a simple assignment, ripping up page after page because they didn't want to submit a paper with an erasure or flaw? For children with NLD, the concept of "good enough" does not exist. Once they learn that there are acceptable efforts between the categories of "perfect" and "garbage," they can minimize homework avoidance and end the Perfection Wars.

From the moment you receive your child's diagnosis and begin to understand the workings of the NLD brain, it is your job to be alert to circumstances which can double as teachable moments. If you learn to weave these moments smoothly into the fabric of daily life, you may be lucky enough to reach the time when your child stops seeing them as pedantic intrusions and actually begins to find validating examples independently. That is the moment when you can take credit for successfully "graying up" your child.

Empirical understanding of the difficulties NLDers face has been greatly enhanced by the recent developments in medical technology. When physicians treating epilepsy began experimenting with split brain surgery for patients with intractable seizures, they took pains to investigate what functions might be diminished if certain areas of the brain were removed. At that time, the attributes that we have come to regard as the assets and deficits of NLD were clearly associated with their origins in either the left or right hemispheres.

The thinking capacities of the left hemisphere were found to be linear and analytic, with a very rational and logical cognitive style. The language of the left brain, as we have noticed in the thoughts and actions of many NLDers, shows competencies in vocabulary, grammar, and syntax. Spatial orientation, when governed by this hemisphere, is relatively poor.

On the other hand, the attributes of the right brain include concrete and holistic thinking, an intuitive and artistic cognitive style, and a metaphoric vocabulary. Right brain thinkers can focus on imagery and *gestalt* perceptions. They also have superior spatial orientation. When both sets of attributes are used concurrently, the deficits are minimized and the brain has tools with which to address most social cognitive situations in an adequate manner. It is important to remember that no two people with NLD are alike. Depending on the unique constellation of assets and deficits of each individual, the level of affectedness in each of the susceptible categories, visual-spatial, sensorimotor, and social, occurs along a continuum. It follows that some NLDers will take to the concept of graying up more easily than others. However arduous the task, this is the one pursuit that can save your children from believing that everything they do is awful. Using NLD logic, that belief engenders the theory that it is not even worth trying to do anything, because failure is a given. We all know where that belief leads.

As studies of the brain have shown us, NLD is a neurological syndrome. Your children do not choose to categorize things only in black and white because it is too annoying to factor in all those other possibilities. They do so simply because they do not have access to the expansive characteristics of the brain's right hemisphere. If you occasionally feel frustrated trying to help them see the world with more flexibility, imagine how frustrated they must feel when they see the way neurotypical children adapt to things with seeming ease and alacrity.

Unfortunately, comparison with others is another area where children with NLD often make inappropriate use of their assets in logical analysis. When they realize that other children arrive at social or academic success with relatively less time and effort than they need, NLDers can become frustrated and distressed at the way the world works for them. This can trigger one of the most difficult consequences of NLD, the loss of confidence and erosion of self-esteem that leads to depression. All of the advocacy work you provide or arrange for your child should be directed at preventing the onset of the negativity and depression that can poison productivity and independence.

Assuming, then, that it is the task of educators, caregivers, healthcare providers, family members, friends, and parents to develop an environment which will help NLDers enjoy the myriad possibilities between perfection and failure, it is imperative that we learn how to undertake this complicated assignment. Essentially, until our children can appreciate the validity of information we are presenting and logically incorporate it into their ways of being, each of us has to function as a surrogate right hemisphere. Although your NLDers may never fully incorporate the right hemisphere functions into their inherent patterns of operation, once they have seen the benefit of using both hemispheres, they will know that they can get help by accessing someone or something that can perform a skill they do not possess.

How would a surrogate right hemisphere function in school? Well, we know that NLDers are fairly good readers, excellent spellers, great repositories of facts and details, and vocabulary champions. What many educators do not realize, however, is that the reading comprehension of most NLDers is not as well developed as their reading fluency, since reading comprehension draws on the right brain for an awareness of the whole picture. A teacher trained to work with our children should know to ask leading questions, to teach content skills methods, and to make sure a student doesn't confuse a verbatim reiteration of the text with an understanding of the nuances and subtleties of the material discussed.

At home, the surrogate frontal lobe might be called upon to counteract frustration caused by homework assignments. The parent or caregiver on homework duty must be very well versed in organizational and study skills, written expression, and problem-solving, for a start. And when Petunia pronounces that she is the stupidest girl in the entire fifth grade, making time for long division becomes less important for the surrogate right hemisphere than applying the social cognitive mechanics of graying up.

Perhaps one of the most difficult tasks for the surrogate right hemisphere is interacting with our NLDers in interpersonal activities. We know that they have impaired social judgment, but we also know that most of them are not aware of their impairments. Helping them develop a sense of appropriate social behavior by gently redirecting errors with suggestions is a delicate task. Since NLDers respond so well to auditory information, the surrogate right hemisphere can also be a guide to body language, facial expression, and intonation.

We know that understanding nonverbal messages is difficult for most NLDers, but many can use auditory coaching to develop personal systems of awareness. NLDers can be effectively coached to recognize nonverbal cues and facial expressions through the use of pictures, television shows, movies, and mirrors. A good surrogate right hemisphere can also help NLDers make effective gains in developing their own facial expressions and verbal prosody.

Teaching your NLDer about the world is a taxing, full-time job. Sometimes you wonder "Is there any time I can get out of teaching mode and just be a parent?" O ye of little faith! That's one of the wonders of this syndrome. Rejoice. NLDers need a lot of sleep. That's when you can relax and just be a regular parent.

Key points

1. The NLDer's tendency to interpret situations as either black or white has both assets and deficits. But categorizing people, events, and emotions as only black or white cuts off a range of possibilities which might make certain situations more tolerable and emotional reactions less difficult to endure. The idea of relative gradations of good and bad has to be carefully and systematically introduced, since at first "graying up" seems like an illogical concept to a person with NLD.

2. From the moment you receive your child's diagnosis and begin to understand the workings of the NLD brain, it is your job to be alert to circumstances which can double as teachable moments. If you learn to weave these moments smoothly into the fabric of daily life, you may witness the occasion when your NLDer understands the concept of "graying up" without external cueing.

3. The message of perfection that NLDers interpret from even the most ingenuous remarks in the world around them is a source of unremitting anxiety.

4. All of the advocacy work you provide or arrange for your child should be directed at preventing the onset of the negativity and depression that can poison productivity and independence.

Chapter Fifteen

Showing and Receiving Love

"I love you sweetie."
"Coo."

"I love you, my little cutie pie."
"Gurgle, glump, goo goo."

"I love you. Have fun at nursery school."
"I love you, too, Mommy."

"Have a great day at school. I love you."
"Jeez…"

"I love you honey. See you after biology."
"Mmmphh."

"Okay, I guess it's time to go.
Daddy's already in the car, so…I
got you this for your dorm, and
here's some money, and here's a
roll of coins for the washing
machine, and there are some extra
lightbulbs in the top drawer,
and…I love you!"
"Dad, could you just move it now?
I mean NOW!"

Is this taxonomy of developmental
affection fundamentally different
for NLDers or does it generally reflect
the patterns of neurotypical children

and adolescents as they grow and achieve healthy separations from their parents? Frankly, if a neurotypical child and an NLDer engaged in the same conversations presented above, each would be considered age appropriate. What is important to evaluate is not *what* is being said at each developmental transition, but *why*.

Although each child with NLD differs from every other, almost all NLDers have difficulty expressing emotions. It follows, then, that love, the emotion most difficult for neurotypicals to understand and express, is even more difficult for NLDers. As the parent of a young man with NLD, I like to believe that feeling love is not a difficult emotion for NLDers. In fact, I truly believe that it is the primary emotion on which human development revolves. But I have come to learn that NLDers express love in different ways to family and friends. They use different physical and expressive vocabularies. Once you learn the language, however, you can feel tightly hugged by your NLD child even if he or she has sensory issues which make physical touch uncomfortable. You can feel as eloquently adored by a one-syllable response from your NLDer as you would by an hour of sonnets from your more oratorical offspring.

You must learn to interpret not only what NLDers do, but also what they do not do, in order to understand how much they care about you, care about others, and appreciate your place in their lives. One NLDer I know does not enjoy the feeling of a hug from either parent. However, when he got old enough to understand what it meant to his parents, he decided to allow them the privilege of hugging him on certain occasions. He no longer defends himself at the appearance of an approaching embrace as though he were about to be beaten with a baseball bat.

Why was it important to desensitize this child to hugging and give him the ability to accept nonsexual human touch without flinching? Well, it certainly helps that undercover agents from the Department of Child and Family Services don't pounce on the parents every time they extend an arm toward their child. But touch is so important that Duke, Nowicki, and Martin (1996) remind us of children in nineteenth-century orphanages who regularly died from a disease called marasmus, which was essentially a lack of human touch. They go on to say that the appropriate interpretation of touch is integral to the development of appropriate social behavior. In fact, the authors conclude that children who misuse or misinterpret touch may experience not only tension and difficulty in their social relations, but even social rejection. It is critical, therefore, that the translation of touch into expression of feeling and other messages begins at home.

In the late 1950s, an experimental psychologist named Harlow began to investigate the biological component of love by experimenting with rhesus monkeys and surrogate mothers. Although modern reviewers claim that some of his experiments unfortunately involved cruelty and pain to animals, none contend with his findings. In his original experiment, a staple of Psychology 101 classes all over the world, Harry Harlow provided infant rhesus monkeys with two types of surrogate mothers, some made of wire, and others covered with soft terrycloth. He showed that even when they received food from the wire surrogate only, all of the babies went to the cloth surrogate for cuddling. Those who were fed by cloth surrogates never even approached the wire model (Harlow and Zimmerman 1959).

Harlow believed that his experiment proved that physical affection was second only to basic sustenance. In later experiments, some of the infants who were deprived of maternal affection actually died. So, for those of us who believe that we are doing our children a favor by acquiescing to their demands for distance, I suggest that we remember Harlow's monkeys.

Touch, however, is certainly not the only way to demonstrate love. Remember that when you want your NLDer to learn something important, you have to repeat the lesson multiple times, use clear and concise language, model the behavior repeatedly, and use every opportunity you can to point out positive instances where the behavior you are discussing occurs. The topic of loving and being loved is so important to your child's basic humanity that you will have to tolerate all sorts of creative deflections, grimaces, and avoidance behaviors that may ensue.

But there is another side to the story of raising children with NLD. We all know that it takes an enormous investment of time and effort to help them find their way along a path which doesn't quite understand their footsteps. At the end of a 24-hour day which seems at least 48 hours long, most parents would like to hear a testament of undying affection or get a wonderful good-night kiss sparkling with a few "I love you"s. It's much more likely that your NLDer will stare purposefully at your face, and just when you expect a declaration of love, you'll hear, "Mom, you're getting a really big pimple on your chin." For those of you who don't have a copy of the NLD dictionary (available only in your heart after years of frustration), this means, "I love you Mom. Thanks for making the world a little easier for me."

Before you are graced with the dictionary download, there are ways to approach the seeming void of returned love you experience when dealing with your NLDer. First, make sure that you have read enough to realize that people with NLD have difficulty understanding and expressing emotions. We recognize expressions of love in other creatures that cannot come right out and say, "I love you." Learn to recognize the way your NLDer expresses love so that you will always understand how much you are appreciated.

When a young man I know well was about to graduate from high school, I was concerned that he might not spontaneously offer a hug to the head of school as most boys have done for all the years I have attended graduation. I was relieved that a few others in his graduating class thought a handshake was more than enough when they received their diplomas, so that this young man would not seem disproportionately ungracious when his name was called. As I had suspected, a hug was indeed not on his agenda. He shook hands, accepted the diploma, displayed what passes for a smile in some circles, and sat down. Weeks later, I was speaking to the head on another matter and expressed my sadness that the young man had been unable to embrace her at graduation. "You are so wrong," she informed me. "You couldn't see from where you were sitting, but he hugged me with his eyes."

In his early work, Byron Rourke suggested that intimate encounters would be all but impossible for NLDers, due to the combination of their inappropriate judgments regarding nonverbal cues and their tactile-perceptual and psychomotor difficulties (Rourke 1989). Happily, the NLD community itself is testament to the error of his predictions. I have met many adults with NLD. Although I have not – nor do I wish to – interrogated them about the quality of their intimate relationships, the fact that some of them have produced children is evidence enough for me that intimate encounters were certainly not impossible.

In today's world, intimate relationships are astonishingly complex. When the rules were simple and inflexible, it was easy to know what was right and what was wrong. Since the 1960s, however, there are so many interpretations of morality that it would be impossible to define the concept to a justice-oriented logical thinker. The best way to approach the subject is to have each family present its own beliefs to its own children, whether they are NLDers or neurotypicals. Our duty as parents is to guide, but not to hound. With NLDers, the questions may be more complicated and challenging, but it's just another aspect of the formidable role we assume when we attempt to make the world accessible to the children we love.

We have learned how to look for love from our NLDers, and we have learned how to help our NLDers find love in relationships with others. In order to make these functions operate smoothly, however, it is most important that we demonstrate love for our NLDers and for all others with whom we are involved in personal relationships. Since NLDers are literal and specific, it is impossible to "talk the talk" if we do not "walk the walk." While others may be able to factor in a few inconsistencies to daily life, NLDers thrive on uniformity and coherence.

You know you love your husband, but your NLDer may not understand why you described him as "the dumbest man who ever walked upright" in a phone conversation with your best friend. The problem with this is that most saints are celibate, and therefore most parents of NLDers are not saints. We make mistakes. We are human. Don't try to be perfect. Believe me, it's grueling. After 50 years, I gave up. So when your NLDers detect an incongruity, explain it. Actually, you'll be relieving some of their anxieties as well as your own. Many NLDers are enslaved by the logical no-nonsense dictatorship of the left brain. It's actually beneficial for them to see that someone can occasionally digress from perfection and still be okay.

So how do we teach love to children who may have sensory issues with touch, problems with expressive language, difficulty accessing and identifying emotions, a tendency toward negativism, pessimism, and depression, fragile self-esteem, and a literal sense of learning that doesn't really make space for intangible, abstract concepts? You'll be surprised to learn that there is a fairly simple way to overcome what seems like a daunting challenge.

Q: How do we teach love to children with NLD?

A: Love them.

Just as we need to reinforce the love we give to neurotypical children with validation they can understand at every age and stage, we need to follow certain rules in order to make sure that our NLDers know that they are loved, that they can develop the confidence to express love, and they will be able to maintain loving relationships throughout life.

- Learn about your child's assets and deficits.

- Listen to your child's needs.

- Examine your family routine for ways to show your child how much he or she is loved.

- Use your child's strongest modality – auditory – to underscore every demonstration of love.

- Use the environment and media to provide examples of love.

- Surround your child with loving relationships among family and friends.

- Even when you are most frustrated with your child's behavior, remember to say that you may not like the behavior, but you always love the child.

- Help your child appreciate the comfort and warmth of a hug or therapeutic touch.

- Don't lose credibility with gratuitous or superficial sentimentality.

- Tell your child "I love you" every day.

Make sure to surround yourself with people who love you and understand the magnitude of your challenges. Loving others starts by loving yourself. Go find someone right now and say, "I love you." You may be absolutely delighted by the response.

Key points

1.   Learn to interpret not only what NLDers do, but also what they do not do, in order to understand how much they care about you, care about others, and appreciate your place in their lives.

2.   Children who misuse or misinterpret touch may experience tension and difficulty in their social relations, or even social rejection. The translation of touch into expression of feeling and other messages must begin at home.

3. Follow the Ten Commandments of Teaching Love to make sure your NLDers can develop the confidence to maintain loving relationships throughout life.

    ○ Learn about your child's assets and deficits.

    ○ Listen to your child's needs.

    ○ Examine family routine for ways to show your children you love them.

    ○ Reinforce every show of love in the auditory modality.

    ○ Use the environment and media to provide examples of love.

    ○ Surround your child with loving relationships among family and friends.

    ○ Even when you are most frustrated with your child's behavior, remember to say that you may not like the behavior, but you always love the child.

    ○ Help your child appreciate the warmth of a hug or therapeutic touch.

    ○ Don't lose credibility with gratuitous or superficial sentimentality.

    ○ Tell your child "I love you" every day.

Chapter Sixteen

Celebrating Success

Since most people with NLD have intelligence scores which fall between the average and superior range, they are usually quite sensitive to any behavior which feels condescending or patronizing. Your well-bred basset hound might sink into obsequious reverie when blessed with "Good job, boy," but it's probably not a good phrase to try on a child with NLD. Since the auditory modality is the way NLDers process knowledge most accurately, it's important to remember that they are highly critical of all information that they receive in this manner. Like sophisticated oenophiles assessing a fine wine, they are the first to know if a few flowers in the verbal bouquet are less than fragrant.

Nevertheless, childhood and early adolescence are critical developmental periods during which NLDers, like their neurotypical peers, formulate and solidify the concept of self that will ultimately be the foundation for adult personalities, attitudes, and aspirations. We all know that people who feel better about themselves are not only happier in daily life, but are generally more successful in all personal and professional pursuits. In fact, a good statistician could probably establish a direct correlation between a person's self-concept and the measure of that person's success at any given task.

As parents and caregivers, we are legally bound to provide our children with food, shelter, and education. Most of us go far beyond the legal requirements and search for the latest developmental theories that assure optimal physical development and health. But although physical health is undeniably important, equally fundamental is the development of a robust and resilient sense of self-esteem, a characteristic which is unfortunately more noticeable when it is shattered than when it is intact.

Children with NLD present a challenge in a world where other children receive praise from all aspects of society for achieving success at expected tasks. Most activities where neurotypicals succeed, like team sports, are usually not areas of great accomplishment for NLDers. We have to make sure to acknowledge the unique and hard-earned successes of NLDers not only at home, but at school and in the community as well. The most important thing is to know your child's assets and deficits and to encourage opportunities for success in areas of inherent capability. Find the area where your child can be a superstar and cheer until your voice is scratchier than nails on a chalkboard.

When NLDers express very clear interests, make sure that you encourage these pursuits with as much time, enthusiasm, and financial support as you can muster. Take your child to museums or exhibits that enhance whatever special interests have developed, and encourage research and projects with the cooperation of teachers at school or in special activities. Make sure that your children are aware of the pride you take in their expertise. Display examples of whatever it is that interests them in your home. Don't forget to tell your NLDers that they should be proud of themselves. Sadly, this is something they tend to miss.

When adolescent NLDers look for summer jobs or part-time positions after school, teach them how to choose environments and tasks which accentuate their assets rather than demonstrate their deficits. Help them prepare for interviews or job fairs, and teach them to enumerate their abilities before describing their weaknesses. In this aspect, NLDers are no different from neurotypical jobseekers. We all have areas of skill and areas of minimal function. Once NLDers realize that they are not the only ones with varying capabilities, they will be able to present their strengths with more confidence and self-esteem.

When your children reach a level of mastery in a certain activity, praise and celebrate, but do not assume that they are ready to move on to the next goal. For people with NLD, change that is introduced forcefully or rapidly is always unwelcome. Allow your NLDer time to enjoy the activity at the level of success which has been achieved. Generalization of this knowledge to the next level of expertise may or may not be possible. If the NLDer ultimately decides to attempt to move forward, that too is a success and a cause for celebration. When you know what your NLDer struggles to achieve, you will know where to give appropriate praise.

When you communicate praise to your NLDer, make sure that your message is clear and direct. Even some of the most articulate NLDers have difficulty understanding figurative language. And if you show your appreciation with body language, tone of voice, or facial expression, it might not register at all. If you are happy about your child's accomplishment, say so. Slapping him on the back while grinning broadly and saying "That's my boy!" might not inform your son how thrilled you were with his accomplishments at the swim meet. He already knows he's your boy. Show all the delight you can display, but when you are through exhilarating, remember to tell your child, "You did a wonderful job today at the swim meet. I'm very proud of all the progress you have made." And most important of all, remind your child that he should relish his own accomplishments. "You should be really proud of yourself. You worked hard for this goal and you really deserve that medal." Since NLDers have difficulty identifying feelings internally, it can often be helpful to load emotions from the outside.

Building self-esteem, however, is not all about praising a child who has done something well. It is also important to build a relationship in which you can tell a child what might be done better without causing pain. Always remember that most of the social errors for which we might want to reprimand a child with NLD are the result of faulty neurology, not volitional bad behavior. Most inappropriate interactions are not planned and executed to elicit a specific reaction or in response to something that has annoyed them earlier. For this reason, it is always ineffective and, in fact, injurious to blame an NLDer for such errors. Instead, discuss why certain behaviors or responses are inappropriate and describe a better way to handle the situation. If your NLDers believe that you have their best interests at heart, this information will be received appreciatively.

Let's continue our afternoon with little Neptune at the swim meet. As proud as you were to see him win the medal, you were somewhat dismayed at his unorthodox acceptance behavior. In case he should have such an honor again, it might be a good idea to help him learn to accept a medal graciously. Start, as always, with the positive, but make sure that you explain what behaviors were wrong, why they were wrong, and what the child can do to correct them.

"It must have been so exciting to hear your name called when they announced the medal winners. I know this was the first one for you, so you probably didn't know exactly how to behave. That must have felt confusing. You probably went with what you thought was cool, but I think it might have been interpreted as a little disrespectful to give the judge a high five and then moon the audience. I think the usual procedure is to shake everyone's hand and then go quietly back to your seat. I really believe that you'll be called up for many more medals this season, so you'll have a chance to show people that you can accept a medal as smoothly as you can swim."

Even when there has been no unusual behavior to correct, you may be surprised to see that your NLDer displays an unusual response to success. There are many possible causes for this. In some cases, public success is a rare experience, and one which causes unusual feelings that the NLDer simply does not know how to handle. Sometimes, a rush of people congratulating an NLDer on a successful accomplishment can cause sensory overload, precipitating a speedy retreat to a less demanding environment. At other times, the NLDer may be experiencing the syndrome-typical tendency to focus on the lone mistake in his performance rather than allowing himself to enjoy the overall success. Whatever the source of atypical behavior, it is your place to help your NLDer sort out the feelings which follow a positive achievement so that he can learn to appreciate success and enjoy the emotions which traditionally accompany it.

One NLDer I know quite well did everything he could to avoid positive interaction with faculty and administrators at his school. Unfortunately, his difficulty calculating long-term consequences thought it might be all right to do well in the national Latin exam, since this had nothing to do with school and would be graded externally. He was right to a point, but the school nevertheless wanted to recognize his successful outcome and awarded him an academic prize. Although he had managed to get through three years of prize ceremonies without being called to the podium, he knew that public acknowledgement was unavoidable this evening. After his name was called, he went up, grabbed the award plaque, and raced back to his seat without a word. Later that evening, in the dorm, he was reported by a teacher for an incident in which he used rude and inappropriate language to a faculty member.

There are many ways to explain this sequence of events. The head of school, although well informed of NLD and its possible sequelae, interpreted it as a planned act of disrespect which was heightened by the subsequent rude interaction with a faculty member. The head suggested that the student was "feeling his oats," "thought he was too good for the school," "didn't think that the rules of etiquette applied to him," "fooled around in the ceremony to mock the seriousness of it," and later "spoke disrespectfully to a teacher because he thought he was such a big shot that there was no distinction between faculty and student at that time."

When a specialist in NLD was asked to review the situation, she explained that the boy was probably terrified at not knowing the procedure for accepting an award. Although he had watched many previous prize ceremonies, he had never generalized the appropriate behavior, and decided to mask his ineptness by clowning around. She suggested that his refusal to shake anyone's hand might look like bravado to the other boys, making him a hero in their eyes, but should really be interpreted as a sign of fear – a way to get away from the podium as quickly as possible. Although the incident later that evening seems related, it was probably coincidental. It was not a planned act of disrespect, but simply another instance of a boy with NLD not knowing how to respond to a faculty member who was seen out of context. Since the teacher was not in the classroom, but had come into the residence hall to ask if he could borrow some toothpaste, the student responded as if he were interacting with another student.

Both interpretations are logical. As it happened, the student was suspended for a week for disrespectful behavior, because schools do have rules and it would be impossible to reinterpret them according to the quirks of each student. Although his family was initially upset, they ultimately realized that NLD should never be used as an excuse in the real world. Ultimately, the incident helped their son realize that it's okay to ask for help when you don't know how to do something. If he had been able to go to his faculty adviser to ask about general procedure for the awards ceremony, all that ensued might have followed a very different course. The parents also used the incident to help their son realize that there are levels of respect in any life situation, whether it is home, school, or work. We don't always respect the people in authority, but even if we want to change things, we must still respect the position.

I sometimes think that it might be wonderful to use the simple logic of NLD reality to deal with problems. Wouldn't it be great in the world of work? That person is my boss. My boss is an idiot. So, it would be stupid to respect my boss's authority and I will not. Actually, I once had to face that situation. Before I opened my private practice, my boss was an idiot. Since I was living in the real world and I used my paycheck for trifles like mortgage payments, child care, food, and education, I didn't have the luxury of deciding not to respect my boss's authority. One day, however, I simply couldn't justify certain things I was asked to do and I resigned. Now I work for myself. If my boss is an idiot, I have only myself to blame.

So what does this have to do with celebrating the success of your NLDer? Everything. Help your child define the boundaries of self in a proactive and protective manner. Make sure that you teach your NLDers about the reality of the world, but never undermine the feelings which define their integrity, morality, and sense of self. Help expose them to situations in which they must challenge their own boundaries. Praise them for their attempts, even when the final results are less than perfect. Teach them to enjoy the journey as well as the destination.

Although success and self-esteem can be ongoing, transportable celebrations, they do not flourish in every climate. For NLDers, these qualities wither in environments which infantilize them or discount their capabilities. Self-esteem self-destructs when your NLDers believe that the praise is gratuitous or superficial. Similarly, they will never be gratified by praise for accomplishments which are below their skill level or intellectual capability. For all of us, self-esteem is a fragile flower, doomed to wilt at the first negative word or hostile glance. But for people with NLD, self-esteem is like a rare orchid. It takes extreme care to tend and nurture, but the ultimate blossom is breathtaking.

Key points

1. People with NLD are highly sensitive to behavior which feels condescending or patronizing. Although NLDers process

knowledge most accurately through the auditory modality, they are highly critical of all information that they receive in this manner.

2.   Some NLDers protect themselves from anxiety and disappointment by trying to subvert success and adopting a negative, pessimistic outlook. This is a self-protective defense, not a character fault.

3.   Self-esteem is not built with praise alone. In order to help NLDers learn to be most appropriate in neurotypical society, parents and caregivers should explain why certain behaviors or responses are inappropriate. In nonjudgmental terms, describe a better way to handle the situation. If your NLDers believe that you have their best interests at heart, this information will be received appreciatively.

4.   It is important for families and caregivers of NLDers to help promote self-esteem and the awareness of success. Celebrating success is an ongoing attitude. In order to facilitate a truly positive sense of self, the celebration of success must pervade the environment of the NLDer's home, school, work, and personal interactions.

Chapter Seventeen

Planning for the Future

Never let the future disturb you. You will meet it, if you have to, with the same weapons of reason which today arm you against the present.

(Marcus Aurelius Antoninus, Meditations, *200 A.D.)*

In the first bonding embrace of mother and child, there are implicit promises and implicit demands. Healthy infants demand to have their needs met – essentially the basic needs for food and human contact, as we learned earlier from our primate pedagogues, Harry Harlow's rhesus monkeys. As societies become more sophisticated, the demands for a clean diaper and a few extremely expensive educational playthings also enter into the relationship.

Emotionally healthy mothers promise unconditionally to meet those demands, but at the same time, they promise almost viscerally to guarantee each baby a life of joy, success, inde-pendence, and productivity. A mother intuitively sees the future in her baby's eyes, and at first glance, it looks divine.

As time passes, and babies become children and adolescents, parents revise the dream. It becomes clear which children will not be opera stars, dancers, artists, or world class athletes. Nev-ertheless, for the parents of neurotypical children, it is possible to adjust the screen of the future *ad*

infinitum as long as nothing intervenes to cataclysmically cancel the possibility of a happy life.

But what does the future hold for children with NLD? Although there are certainly many adult NLDers functioning quite competently in the world today, very few are aware of the diagnosis. Those who do have a definite diagnosis represent such a small number that it would be impossible to extract significant patterns from their successes and their challenges. Children living with NLD today are the promise of NLD tomorrow. They will help clarify the path to success, the pitfalls, and the successful accommodations.

It becomes critically important, then, for parents, educators, healthcare providers, and caregivers to understand what we can do for children with NLD that will optimize their neurological, academic, behavioral, social, emotional, and personal development. It is up to us to refute the prognoses of early theorists who condemned NLDers to depression and underemployment in adult life. And there is no need to begin our research in laboratories for developmental psychology or in state of the art facilities for neuroscience. We must begin in our homes, one child at a time.

As I have mentioned frequently, there are parts of life in which you can control the environment to meet your child's specific assets and deficits. It is much more effective in the long run, however, if you help your child adjust to the demands of a world created for neurotypicals. For example, you know how your child struggles to transition from sleep to wakefulness, but most employers are not sympathetic to, "Oh, I know I'm supposed to be here at nine, but I have NLD, and it's really hard for me to wake up, so I usually get in around ten-thirty."

For younger children, schools which start later or have flexible morning periods are wonderful; but as our NLDers approach maturity, it is important to help them realize that they might have to implement some long-term planning strategies and learn to take control of things which affect their lives. An effective long-term strategy might lead them to realize that classes scheduled later in the day, flex-time, second-shift jobs, or self-employment are more productive choices. It is important, however, to recognize the process by which the decision is made, and that successful life plans do not occur by happenstance or default.

Always remember who your child is when you are helping to make plans that will impact on the future. Some children with NLD recognize their assets and accept their deficits. But these are uncommon representatives of the syndrome. Most suffer from *anosognosia*, the inability to understand the seriousness of their problems or diagnosis. It would be painful and inappropriate to tell them, "You have to do it this way because you are neurologically impaired. Listen to me. I'm only doing this for your own good." But you can be programmatically effective and much, much kinder if you say, "Gosh you're such a zombie in the morning! Wouldn't it be great if we could try to set up a class schedule that started at noon? Maybe they could help arrange that in the Office of Academic Advising."

In many families with a child who has NLD, there are those who understand the syndrome and its ramifications and those who believe that the NLDer is actually being lazy, manipulative, childish, uncooperative, or simply disagreeable. Such rifts can leave NLDers with permanent deficits in self-concept and confidence. The resentment they feel, whether implicit or overt, inhibits the feeling of support that is the foundation of adult emotional stability. Since NLDers don't always have friends from whom they can derive support, a united front at home is truly critical.

We all know that many children don't get everything they need from their parents. That is reality. Let's face it, that is also the source of income for many who practice the art and science of psychiatry. But the reality of helping NLDers arrive at productive adulthood is that most neurotypical parents are able to actively do something to remove whatever obstacles they are causing. When there is a child with NLD in the family, obligations are non-negotiable and expectations must be clear and direct. Parents who have different opinions about a child need to work out a mutually acceptable presentation that is consistent in all family matters.

Family meetings should be held with siblings so that no one harbors resentment because of misperceptions about an NLDer's responsibilities. Learning-disability coaches and psychologists familiar with NLD often see families on a regular basis to advise on ongoing issues, to coach families on approaching future issues, and to problem-solve for issues that the family cannot resolve themselves. Getting help does not mean there is something wrong with the family. It means there is something right about the way they are guaranteeing a healthy future for their NLDer.

In helping children and adolescents prepare for life outside the family, it is critically important to help the NLDer understand the role that language plays in adapting to "outside" life. Like everything else in this complex syndrome, it can be both an asset and a deficit. Because many NLDers speak early and develop extensive vocabularies at a young age, they are often considered more competent and mature than they actually are. Some use their language strengths as a defensive bravado which occasionally gets them into situations they find frightening and incomprehensible. Ironically, people who judge NLDers by their language skills are often the first to condemn them as oppositional, because they refuse to believe that a child who seems so bright cannot do some of the things that truly incapacitate an NLDer.

On the other hand, language, both expressive and receptive, is the medium through which children and adults with NLD construct the reality of the world in which they live. By teaching them to talk through tasks that seem initially confusing, you can help them learn how to ground themselves and reduce anxiety that might interfere with task completion. You should also teach NLDers a set of social tools or scripts which they can access in recurring situations.

Although most NLDers are unable to generalize, they can recognize a situation, and remember that they have a script which will make access to this situation easier. There may be an imperceptible delay as they remind themselves, "Oh, I have to remember what I am supposed to do here, wait a minute, this is a cocktail party. I remember, I should go up to someone, smile, say hello, then go over to the *hors d'oeuvres* table, do the same, get a drink or a snack, and repeat until a longer conversation develops." It may seem incomprehensible to some of us that there are people who need reminders for social behaviors that are so intuitive to others. But that is exactly the key. They are intuitive to others, not to NLDers.

Once NLDers initiate the activity, they can generally continue, but the prompt has not been programmed into their behavioral intuition. Teaching them scripts in nonjudgmental ways as they mature can help them jumpstart appropriate interactions. Once they get where they are going, no one will know how long it took them to warm up the engine.

I recently had a conversation with a man who had been sent to Turkey during his service with the U.S. Navy. He explained how the education officer informed all the sailors about particular foibles of Turkish customs and culture before they landed so that representatives of the U.S. Navy would not be considered socially illiterate boors. When you give your NLDers a set of behavioral guides for the neurotypical world, you are performing a similar task. In this case, however, you are ensuring that they do not represent *themselves* as socially illiterate boors.

NLDers may be proficient at using words that are superficially sound, but they often have difficulty finding the right words to express their own feelings. Most NLDers translate their feelings into non-specific generalized anxiety. Parents and caregivers can equip NLDers with great advocacy skills for the future by teaching them to recognize and express such feelings as "I feel overwhelmed when I have a big paper due and it's very hard for me to get started," or "I feel nervous when I need new clothes because the big stores make me so uncomfortable."

By knowing the source of the anxiety, we can help our NLDers develop constructive accommodations before the anxiety turns into frustration and despair. As they mature and become independent, it will help them immensely to recognize, "Oh, here's that feeling I get whenever I have a paper assigned. I'll probably feel better if I go over to the writing center a few weeks before the final deadline to get some guidelines about setting up my work."

The greatest disability in the NLD syndrome is anxiety. It can lead to frustration, depression, fear of trying new things, of going new places, and of meeting new people. When children and adults with NLD fear that they may encounter a situation that will tax their social, academic, or emotional repertoire, their natural default is to withdraw. In some extreme cases, this withdrawal leads to a reclusive, lonely, and unhappy existence. This is the most extreme and dire consequence of NLD and the one that all of us who love an NLDer want to know how to prevent.

Like everything else connected to this syndrome, there is no quick answer. The process is as slow as the processors themselves. But we must always remember that, although people with NLD process slowly and in unique and individual styles, they do process. We never know when the "Aha!" moment will occur, but it is definitely the direct result of intensive, extensive practice and unremitting optimism.

One adult with NLD, who is successful professionally as a statistician and successful socially as a husband and father, characterizes his own developing awareness of his issues:

> *Stage One – Up to Age 11*
> There's nothing wrong with ME. There must be something wrong with YOU.
>
> *Stage Two – Adolescence*
> There's something wrong with me. Leave me alone. Go away. I hate you, me, and everyone else. Life sucks. Maybe I'll jump out a window.
>
> *Stage Three – College to Age 22*
> There's something wrong with me, but it isn't the end of the world, but I can't possibly tell anyone 'cause…
>
> *Stage Four – Age 22 to 30*
> There's something wrong with me, and I better tell everyone I know, even people I don't know, so they will know how mature I am, and that they had better make allowances for me, and treat me special.
>
> *Stage Five – Age 30 to present (40s, still developing)*
> There's something wrong with me, it's up to me to cope with it, so I better have a sense of humor about it.
>
> *(Flom 2003)*

All of us who worry about the future of NLDers can take heart from Peter Flom's thoughts about Stage Six. With curiosity, optimism, and enthusiasm, he asks, "I wonder what it will be like?" There is a future for children, adolescents, and adults with NLD. It is our responsibility, however, to make sure that the wonder out-trumps the worry.

By building a stairway to the future step by step, we can guarantee that the NLDers with who it is our privilege to interact will be able to acquire the energy and enthusiasm they need, at the pace they need, and with the awareness they need. And we, the people who love them, will be able to embrace their futures as we did the day they were born, remembering gratefully the words of W. Somerset Maugham, who wrote in 1915:

Life wouldn't be worth living if I worried over the future as well as the present.

(Maugham 1992)

Key points

1. Children living with NLD today are the promise of NLD tomorrow. We must learn how to optimize their neurological, academic, behavioral, social, emotional, and personal development in order to refute the prognoses of early theorists who condemned NLDers to depression and underemployment in adult life.

2. Language, both expressive and receptive, is the medium through which children and adults with NLD construct the reality of the world in which they live. By teaching them to talk through tasks that seem initially confusing, you can help them learn how to ground themselves and reduce anxiety that might interfere with task completion. You should also teach NLDers a set of social tools or scripts which they can access in recurring situations.

3. NLDers often have difficulty finding the right words to express their own feelings. Most NLDers translate their feelings into non-specific generalized anxiety. Parents and caregivers can equip NLDers with great advocacy skills for the future by teaching them to recognize and express such feelings.

4. The greatest disability in the NLD syndrome is anxiety, which can lead to frustration, depression, withdrawal, fear of trying new things, of going new places, and of meeting people. In some extreme cases, this can lead to a reclusive and unhappy existence, a dire consequence of NLD and the one that all of us who love an NLDer want to know how to prevent.

Chapter Eighteen

From Fantasy to Reality

There is no way to prevent the ultimate collision of an NLDer with the real world. Reality does not discriminate against the age of diagnosis, the severity of symptoms, the gentleness of spirit, the strength of intellect, or the purity of heart. The real world asks all who approach its domain, "Can you do this task efficiently? Can you deliver this product optimally? Can you deal with this problem effectively?" Those who hesitate, for any reason or justification, are asked to step out of line.

As we all know, it is probably better for children and adults with NLD to step far away from a line which judges them only by activities that are better performed by neurotypicals. We have stressed throughout that NLDers march to their own unique pace, to the tune of a different drummer. But most of the world operates on neurotypical time, by neurotypical rules, and with a neurotypical view of productivity. Since NLDers are a minority in the neurotypical world, they must learn to understand the rules of neurotypical society in order to carry out their daily life tasks without roadblocks. They must find ways to circumvent derision, bullying, and loss of self-esteem, to earn a living wage, and to maintain the social interaction which is the foundation of a healthy life.

A world where NLDers can accomplish these tasks with relative ease seems so far in the future that it feels almost like fantasy. Nevertheless, it is the goal of every person connected to the NLD community to help make the way to the world accessible for people with NLD. The idea of having people with NLD lead independent, productive lives should be reclassified, from fantasy to reality.

Before that can happen, there are many changes which need to be assimilated into all levels of society, including the academic, professional, and ordinary interactions of daily life. When the hopes and dreams of today become the accepted expectations of tomorrow, the way to the world for people with NLD will be a clearly defined path instead of a precipitous incline. If we expect to turn the hopes and dreams of today into the reality of tomorrow, we must first define them, prioritize them, and work together to activate them.

The primary important advances for NLD will begin empirically, in the field of testing. Not only will diagnosis become clear and expedient, but it will also enable professionals to assess the specific categories of assets and deficits of each individual with NLD. When such definition is available, NLDers will be able to approach the real world with a clear understanding of their capabilities and, equally important, a realistic awareness of areas in which they are not likely to be successful.

Access to such individually specific information will save a great deal of time, humiliation, and frustration in the world of work. Furthermore, it could give NLDers an indication of what fields to follow when there are academic, career, or vocational decisions to make. The entire cycle of failure and depression could ultimately be avoided by following a path which has been empirically supported as feasible by valid and reliable testing.

If diagnosis and specific definition of learning styles, strengths, and preferences are clarified early in the NLDer's life, the entire academic experience at school can be developed on a proactive and positive foundation. Too many NLDers go through school today without understanding why the knowledge in their brains does not translate to anything acceptable to classroom teachers. When teachers of the future understand NLD as clearly as they do dyslexia, they will set their expectations to recognize both our children's assets and their deficits.

As we mentioned much earlier in this journey, when children leave the safe, ego-boosting environment of home to go to school, they have the first sustained opportunity to compare themselves to others. Even more important, they give others the first opportunity to compare them to whatever norm the psychological community has dictated for that day or decade. We know that the NLD brain defaults to disaster. When NLDers see someone who ties shoelaces faster, jumps higher, or reads better, they do not assume that each person is unique and each has wonderful qualities. They assume that the others are "good" and they are "bad."

Without the knowledge that NLD is simply one way of doing things, NLDers begin to develop a sense of inferiority from an early age. But NLDers of the future may simply be recognized as regular, ordinary kids who just do things a little differently.

Perhaps a kindergarten teacher of the future will make some mental notes as she scans her new pupils on a crisp fall day.

"Mmhmm, there are the Fresser twins. Their mother told me to make sure they get equal portions of their snack or World War III will erupt. Oh, there's that pretty little redhead whose picture I saw in the intake files. Yeah, there's the Stilton boy. I have to remember to have him wait at dismissal. He walks home with his older brother who stays after school for student council. The brother must be some sort of big cheese in the sixth grade. And that cute one with the crewcut must be the boy with NLD. I'll just make a note to give him a few more minutes to get organized so he won't feel stressed when we pack up. And over there, that must be…"

Before we can enroll our young NLDers in that fantasy kindergarten of the future, we have a lot of work to do in the arena of public and professional information. Although it seems inconceivable to me, I still meet pediatricians, psychologists, psychiatrists, and educators who are unaware of NLD or who have only the most cursory knowledge of the syndrome and its ramifications. Because NLDers themselves are all so different, it is difficult to develop a diagnostic model which is not ridiculously inclusive or arbitrarily exclusive.

While the scientists are fighting over symptoms and terminology, I have developed a diagnostic measure which has a 100 per cent accuracy rate. Unfortunately, some of its components are a bit unorthodox and unwieldy for modern medical practice, but I still contend that it is foolproof. In order to make a diagnosis of NLD, simply invite a physician or psychiatrist to spend a few days in the home of the suspected NLDer and family. If, during the time enjoyed there, the diagnostician does not witness a predetermined amount of classic NLD moments, then everyone can go back to the manuals to search for another diagnosis. NLD is not an occult disorder. It is a living, breathing, way of life which manifests itself for 24 hours out of each day of an NLDer's life.

Once people accept and understand the syndrome's occurrence and prevalence, people with NLD and the people who share their lives will have access to clinicians, educators, and therapists of all kinds who know exactly how to help them. The occupational therapy community has been in the forefront of recognizing what helps people with NLD, but relatively few psychiatrists and psychologists are aware of therapies that facilitate change and alleviate anxiety and depression for NLDers.

The syndrome is under-represented at professional conferences, in professional journals, and in community and social groups. Even friends and neighbors who can support a family's struggles with a child's diagnosis of AD/HD or dyslexia are totally clueless when NLD is mentioned. In fact, many families sadly notice that their social groups diminish to only people who understand why they have to worry about such a good-looking bright child.

Part of the worrying that we do for children and young adults with invisible disabilities is generated by the fact that there is so little formal intervention available in most communities. NLDers, even those who seem mildly affected in each category, need support and guidance at every stage of life. Just as the impairment varies, so does the degree of support; but the need for support can rarely be eliminated. From early childhood through the adult years, NLDers can benefit from supportive guidance and reinforcement in social skills, academic and organizational skills, and employment decisions and job-search skills. They are also receptive to the right kind of framework for helping them adapt to transitions involving people, places, and emotions.

The emotions that NLDers experience are no different from the feelings of neurotypicals. They are simply processed in a different way. In order for helping professionals to be effective with NLDers, they must be non-judgmental, optimistic, and familiar with NLD-specific processing paths. Perhaps one day counselor training will include coursework on effective modalities for working with NLDers, just as therapists studying today are trained to work with people diagnosed with depression or obsessive compulsive disorder. And every professional working with NLDers must completely believe that they have the potential to be superstars.

When there are after-school groups for NLDers, community center pre-sentations for families about NLD, television programs about NLDers over-coming their difficulties to achieve success, and ongoing familiarity with the syndrome in general society, perhaps the most painful and damaging behavior of neurotypical society toward children and adults with NLD will begin to diminish.

Bullying is the factor most often cited by adults and children with NLD as the most devastating experience of their school careers. What are the reasons which make our children so susceptible to bullying and what can we do to remove them from the victim category in the future? Ironically, children with NLD who have not been trained to deflect the hostile aggres-sions of a bully are actually made-to-order victims for harassment. Bullies seek victims who are typically anxious, insecure, and suffer from low self-esteem. They prefer to pick on people who are safe targets, unlikely to defend themselves or retaliate. It is often easier for a bully to choose a victim who is socially isolated, since there is no need to contend with a group of friends who might come to the victim's aid (Batsche and Knoff 1994).

As if contending with a bully weren't enough, the few friends that our NLDers might have made at school will probably desert them once they have been identified as targets of bullies, for fear of being included in the grand scheme of harassment. The emotional default that our children often use when confronted with confusing emotional decisions takes over and leads almost directly to a lowering of self-esteem and depression. Some children are so afraid to report the bully for fear of retaliation that they report symptoms of physical illness, or find excuses not to take the school bus. Some even refuse to go to school at all.

It is astonishing to think that one bully can completely rob a child of his or her right to a stress-free learning environment. Unfortunately, this is often the case, and not only where NLDers are involved. But NLDers in particular, no matter how bright they may be, generally lag behind their peers in social development. To make matters worse, they often find them-selves without a group of friends upon whom they can rely for support. As a result, they are unable to develop the cognitive and emotional strength to understand that words cannot hurt them or that perhaps the bully has emo-tional or developmental reasons for acting so badly. Their fear of bullies operates at a level of cognitive and relational awareness much younger than what might be appropriate for their chronological age.

One middle schooler was so afraid of consistent verbal taunting on the bus that he put a large kitchen knife in his backpack. He intended to tell the bully, "Don't start up with me because I have a knife in my bag and I can defend myself." Luckily, there was no bullying on the bus that morning and the student had no need to mention the knife. When he got to school, however, he remembered that having a weapon on school grounds was cause for expulsion. He approached the teacher on bus duty, pulled the knife out of his bag, and said, "Could you hold this for me until it's time to go home? I don't need it in school. It's only for the bus."

Would you believe such naïveté if you didn't understand the mindset of NLD? The teacher did not. The vice principal did not. The boy was expelled and he never understood why. When asked to intervene, I explained that he had definitely made a wrong decision to take a knife on the bus, even though he never intended to use it, but that the worst decision had been made by the school when they decided to expel him. If they had understood NLD logic, they would have expelled the bully, not the victim.

In a reality that recognizes and supports NLD, the bullies will not only be expelled, but will be counseled, educated, and ultimately return to school as advocates of the underdog. But before we put too much fantasy spice into the flavor of future reality, it's important to consider the issue of social acceptance, a topic which has been mentioned by every NLDer and parent of an NLDer who has ever discussed the future with me. Although many NLDers have no external identifying characteristics, people who spend time with them will learn to recognize certain patterns and behaviors which definitely originate from their neurological differences. These stem from the three affected categories, visual-spatial, sensorimotor/organizational, and social.

Some NLDers speak slowly, some process slowly, some do everything slowly! Others are not noticeably slower than their neurotypical peers, but they are rigid about certain behavioral patterns, and resistant to novelty or change. It may be hard to encourage them to try a new activity or route. All of us, neurotypical or not, are set in our ways; but since NLDers are in the minority, most people don't understand why they do the things they do in the ways that they do. When people know more about NLD, perhaps certain NLD behaviors won't seem so odd.

When I was a senior in college, I tore a tendon in my leg during a particularly rowdy scene in the orientation play. (After all, it was the 1960s!) It took me forever to get around campus on crutches, but my friends adjusted to my pace because they understood why I was hobbling, they still loved me because I was smart and funny, and they wanted to make me feel better by staying at my side when things were difficult. That is exactly what I would wish for NLDers of the future. At their orientation to the world, they get hobbled in a few areas. But they get compensated in others. So, we hope, people who understand all about NLD (and there will be many!) will know exactly where they fall short and where they excel and will love them for the quirkiness of the combination.

Kelli Bond is the creator and administrator of an online support group for parents and family members of people with NLD, teens and adults with NLD, and the people who care about them (NLD-In-Common@ yahoogroups.com). Her dreams for the new reality, including a close family member with NLD, are inspiring:

> I see the day where more teachers will *find* the many places, hidden and obvious, where students with NLD and related conditions can *lead* in the classroom, the school, and the larger community. Yes, *lead*. Just as basic social skills can be taught, so can leadership (a collection of the most advanced social skills). The latter, blended with the NLD quest for inclusiveness born of frequent exclusion, many an NLDer's stone-solid sense of right and wrong, the often-burning desire to be of service and the inextinguishable NLD verbal-conceptual firepower, could produce our next Martin Luther King, Jr., Mother Teresa, Gandhi, or even that child's most beloved gentle giant of a schoolteacher from a few years back. The level of renown is unimportant. What's important is opportunity – plenty of it. To actively mine those leadership venues and platforms for our NLDers is to begin the long-overdue erosion of the idea that only popularity (and, all too often, mediocrity) can win.

> *(Bond 2003)*

Long before popular divas found it trendy to study the Kabbalah, ancient Jewish mysticism was explored through the rabbinic practice of

Gematriyah, in which each letter of the Hebrew alphabet was assigned a numerical value. Scholars then compared words and passages for numerical similarity to see if they could develop intricate allegorical networks of meaning. This method of Biblical exegesis was arduous and time-consuming, but it laid the foundation for some astonishingly elaborate explanations of Scripture.

Alas, no matter how long we search, I don't think we will find the answers to our questions about NLD in ancient texts or mystical methodology. But as I search for the way to end my work on a meaningful note, it must be more than mere coincidence that I conclude with Chapter 18. According to the Rules of Gematriyah, the number eighteen is formed by two Hebrew letters, *cheth* and *yod*, the eighth and tenth characters in the Hebrew alphabet. Together these two letters form the word for "Life."

I can think of no better way to embody the sum of hopes and dreams for people with NLD and the people who love them.

To Life!

Key points

1. Since NLDers are a minority in the neurotypical world, they must learn to understand the rules of neurotypical society in order to carry out their daily life tasks without roadblocks. They must find ways to circumvent derision, bullying, and loss of self-esteem, to earn a living wage, and to maintain the social interaction which is the foundation of a healthy life.

2. Without the knowledge that NLD is simply one way of doing things, NLDers begin to develop a sense of inferiority from an early age. But NLDers of the future may be lucky enough to be recognized as regular, ordinary people who just do things a little differently.

3. NLD is not an occult disorder. It is a living, breathing, way of life which manifests itself for 24 hours out of each day of an NLDer's life. Once people accept and understand the syndrome's occurrence and prevalence, people with NLD and

the people who share their lives will have access to clinicians, educators, and therapists of all kinds who know exactly how to help them.

4.   NLDers experience the same feelings as neurotypicals. They simply process them differently. Helping professionals who are effective with NLDers must be nonjudgmental, optimistic, and familiar with NLD-specific processing paths.

References

American Optometric Association (AOA) (1997) *Position Statement of Optometric Vision Therapy. Definition of Optometric Vision Therapy.* St Louis, MO: AAO. www.aoanet.org

Batsche, G.M. and Knoff, H.M. (1994) "Bullies and their victims: Understanding a pervasive problem in the schools." *School Psychology Review 23,* 2, 165–74.

Blim, L. (2003) Personal writing used with permission of the author.

Bond, K. (2003) Personal correspondence between the author and Kelli Bond, creator and administrator, NLD-In-Common Online Support Group. Used with permission of the author.

Carroll, L. (2002) *The Complete Stories and Poems of Lewis Carroll.* New York, NY: Gramercy.

Duke, M., Nowicki, S. and Martin, E. (1996) *Teaching Your Child the Language of Social Success.* Atlanta, GA: Peachtree Publishers, Ltd.

Flom, P. (2002) Personal writings published with permission of the author.

Flom, P. (2003) Personal writings published with permission of the author.

Gilbert, W.S. (2000) *H.M.S. Pinafore.* Mineola, NY: Dover Publications.

Greene, R.W. (1998) *The Explosive Child: A New Approach for Understanding and Parenting Easily Frustrated, Chronically Inflexible Children.* New York, NY: HarperCollins.

Greenspan, S. (1995) *The Challenging Child.* New York, NY: Kluwer Academic/Plenum Publishers.

Harlow, H.F. and Zimmerman, R.R. (1959) "Affectional responses in the infant monkey." *Science 130,* 421–32.

Johnson, D.J. and Myklebust, H.R. (1967) *Learning Disabilities: Educational Principles and Practices.* New York, NY: Grune & Stratton.

The KID Foundation (2003) The Foundation for Knowledge in Development. 1901 West Littleton Blvd., Littleton, CO 80120.

Kranowitz, C.S. (1998) *The Out-of-Sync Child.* New York, NY: Perigee.

Kübler-Ross, E. (1997) *On Death and Dying: What the Dying Have to Teach Doctors, Nurses, Clergy, and Their Own Families.* New York, NY: Scribner.

Lavoie, R. (2002) *Social Tips for Giving and Receiving Gifts.* www.RickLavoie.com/holidaysart.html

Lavoie, R. (2003) *On the Waterbed: The Impact of LD on the Family.* www.RickLavoie.com.

Maugham, W.S. (1992) *Of Human Bondage.* New York, NY: Penguin USA.

Meltzer, B. (1982) *Meltzer's Guidance for Living.* New York, NY: Doubleday.

NORD – National Organization for Rare Disorders, Inc. www.rarediseases.org

Rourke, B.P. (1989) *Nonverbal Learning Disabilities: The Syndrome and the Model.* New York, NY: The Guilford Press.

Rourke, B.P. (ed.) (1995) *Syndrome of Nonverbal Learning Disabilities: Neurodevelopmental Manifestations.* New York, NY: The Guilford Press.

Sullivan, H.S. (1953) *The Interpersonal Theory of Psychiatry.* New York, NY: Horton.

Thompson, S. (1997) *The Source for Nonverbal Learning Disorders.* East Moline, IL: Linguisystems.

Thompson, S. (1998) "Neurobehavioral Characteristics Seen in the Classroom: Developing an Educational Plan for the Student with NLD." The Gram, LDA-CA, San Francisco: Publication of the East Bay Learning Disabilities Association.

Thoreau, H.D. (1969) *The Portable Thoreau, Revised Edition.* New York, NY: The Viking Press.

Tolstoy, L. (1997) *Anna Karenina.* Harmondsworth, UK: Penguin Books, Ltd.

Twain, M. (1997) *When In Doubt, Tell the Truth.* Collins, B. (ed.) New York, NY: Columbia University Press.

Wiener, J. and Schneider, B.H. (2002) "Multisource exploration of the friendship patterns of children with and without learning disabilities." *Journal of Abnormal Child Psychology 30,* 2, 127–41.

Subject Index

Author Index

American Optometric Association (AOA) 165

Batsche, G.M. 210
Blim, L. 124
Bond, K. 212

Carroll, L. 147

Duke, M. 180

Flom, P. 31, 204
Fulghum, R. 92

Gilbert, W.S. 61
Greene, R.W. 37
Greenspan, S. 170, 180

Harlow, H.F. 187, 199

Johnson, D.J. ·31

The KID Foundation 75
Knoff, H.M. 210
Kohlberg, L. 143
Kranowitz, C.S. 80, 89, 141
Kübler-Ross, E. 61

Lavoie, R. 59, 129

Martin, E. 180
Maugham, W.S. 204–5
Meltzer, B. 176
Myklebust, H.R. 31

Nowicki, S. 180

Rourke, B.P. 9, 13, 28, 31, 34, 86, 119, 153, 155, 188

Schneider, B.H. 176
Shaw, G.B. 59
Sullivan, H.S. 175–6

Thompson, S. 41, 89
Thoreau, H.D. 29
Tolstoy, L. 70
Twain, M. 126

Wiener, J. 176

Zimmerman, R.R. 187